The
PRIORITY
LIST

A Teacher's Final Quest to Discover
Life's Greatest Lessons

DAVID MENASCHE

A Touchstone Book
Published by Simon & Schuster

New York   London   Toronto   Sydney   New Delhi

Touchstone
A Division of Simon & Schuster, Inc.
1230 Avenue of the Americas
New York, NY 10020

First Touchstone hardcover edition January 2014

TOUCHSTONE and colophon are
registered trademarks of Simon & Schuster, Inc.

For information about special discounts for bulk purchases,
please contact Simon & Schuster Special Sales at
1-866-506-1949 or business@simonandschuster.com.

The Simon & Schuster Speakers Bureau can bring authors
to your live event. For more information or to book an event,
contact the Simon & Schuster Speakers Bureau at 866-248-3049
or visit our website at www.simonspeakers.com.

Interior design by Ruth Lee-Mui

1   3   5   7   9   10   8   6   4   2

Library of Congress Cataloging-in-Publication data is available.

ISBN 978-1-9821-5812-5
ISBN 978-1-4767-4346-2 (ebook)

To Jacques Menasche,
who taught me that there was
no need to be brave and then showed me how to be.

THE PRIORITY LIST

Prologue

Allow me, if you will, to borrow the words of the great Lou Gehrig in his farewell speech at Yankee Stadium, shortly after being told at thirty-six years old that he was looking at the end of his life. *Today, I consider myself the luckiest man on the face of the earth.*

I do, and I am.

I was around the same age as Lou when, in 2006 and at the pinnacle of my teaching career, I was diagnosed with a brain tumor and given months to live. It is seven years later and as I sit here in my home in New Orleans, crippled and nearly blind, I feel lucky that I am still able to appreciate the beauty of the pink magnolias outside my window, and behold my loved ones, and laugh with my friends, and have this chance to share my story.

I am realistic. There is no reason I should still be alive.

The disease never lets me forget that *it*, and not I, will ultimately win this battle of wills. I know the cancer will have its way, and sooner rather than later.

But as my vision diminishes and my world grows dark, as my arms weaken to the point where I can no longer lift a fork to feed myself, and my legs wither beneath me, I have chosen to spend what limited time I have in the only way I know how. With joy.

I can no longer command a classroom, as I once did. But my hope is by sharing my experiences and lessons, especially as I die, that others will be reminded of the preciousness of life. I have never appreciated it more than now when I have so little time left.

And again, I borrow from baseball's Iron Horse in his farewell speech:

So I close in saying that I may have had a tough break, but I have an awful lot to live for.

Until I cease to breathe, I will.

1

My left ear buzzed. I didn't think much of it, except that it was as irritating as one of those pesky gnats that ride your head like a Wave Swinger at an amusement park. Only this buzzing was *inside* my head. I tried ignoring it, until one day, a few months after it started, the sound turned into a tremor that ran from my face, all the way down the left side of my body, and later to the tip of my toes. *Time to see a doctor, Menasche,* I told myself. Paula made the appointment. She took care of anything in our marriage that involved organization. Without Paula, the lights would go out before I remembered that the electric bill hadn't been paid.

I went to my general practitioner, who sent me to an ear, nose, and throat guy, who decided I needed to see a neurologist. His name was Dr. Paul Damski. He was young, not much more than my age at the time, thirty-four, and he seemed cool and direct. My kind of guy. I was hoping he'd chalk up my symptoms to a pinched nerve or a nervous tic, but instead he ordered a battery of tests. All of them had acronyms. EEG. EKG. CAT. MRI. I felt a huge sense of relief when the first three came back okay. The last one, the MRI, magnetic resonance imaging, was certain to tell a story, Dr. Damski said. I'd have to wait a few days for the outcome. No one likes the waiting part and I'm no exception. So I concentrated on the one thing I knew could occupy my mind in the meantime. I threw myself into my job.

Coral Reef Senior High is called Miami's mega magnet school for good reason. Students from all over the country compete to get into one of the six preparatory academies—International Baccalaureate, Agriscience and Engineering, Business and Finance, Legal and Public Affairs, Health Sciences, and Visual and Performing Arts. Selection is based on a lottery, except for the Visual and Performing Arts Academy. Those students have to audition to get in, and the competition is fierce. With so many aspiring performers, the atmosphere is a lot like what you see in the movie *Fame*. Girls and boys are always practicing songs and dance steps in the hallways. You just could not help but be in a good mood when you were there. Until I got sick, I had never missed a day.

I was one of the original staff when the school opened in 1997. It was my first teaching job, and honestly, at twenty-five, I wasn't much older than my students. I spent most of my sixteen years there teaching eleventh-grade honors and advanced placement English. I loved watching these fifteen- and sixteen-year-olds grapple with their first major life decisions—future careers, relationships, where to live, which colleges to attend, and what to study—at the same moment they're learning to drive, getting their first jobs, and experimenting with drugs, alcohol, sex, identity, and freedom. It's a transcendental time for kids. Miraculously, even though they're beginning to gain independence and are often eager for more, most aren't sick of school yet. And I felt very privileged to be part of their metamorphoses.

One way I tried to signal my eagerness to not be just another teacher to these kids was to have my classroom be always open. There were usually a half dozen to a dozen students who hung out there during lunchtime. Many days, someone would be rehearsing lines or singing or dancing, or playing the violin or guitar. Except for the times when a student came in crying over a boyfriend or a bad grade, and that was usually before or after school, it was a jubilant environment.

That's how it was the day I got my diagnosis.

It was the day before Thanksgiving, my favorite holiday. I was sitting at my desk with my best work friend, Denise Arnold, who taught senior honors English. Denise is petite and eats like a bird. When she did eat, it was usually a few M&M's from a bag she kept stashed in her desk. I'd usually buy something healthy at lunchtime and try to shame her into taking a few bites. That day we were splitting a salad from the cafeteria and kidding about how lucky we were because this time we got cucumber with our plastic container of wilted iceberg lettuce and soggy croutons. Kids were milling in and out. As we were finishing up, my cell phone rang with the ringtone from the old Mario Brothers video game. I flipped it open and saw my doctor's number on the screen.

"Hello?" I said, standing up from my desk.

"This is Dr. Damski's nurse practitioner," the voice at the other end of the phone said plaintively. "Your test results are in."

I guess it's my optimistic nature, but I'm always expecting things will turn out okay. "Oh," I said cheerily. "Great! What are they?"

She hesitated just long enough that I felt my heart quiver. "No," she said. "You need to come in. And you need to bring someone with you."

I felt like she'd kicked me in the gut. "I'm in school and I can't get there until later," I said.

Fear really plays games with your head. I think I was hoping that by saying I couldn't get there right away—by holding on to the normalcy of my life before that phone call—I could make the outcome different. That the nurse practitioner would say, *Oh, no problem, let's schedule for another time.* She didn't.

"Don't worry about the time," she said. "The doctor will stay."

Now she was kicking me in the gut with cleats on.

"Okay," I said.

I snapped my phone closed and turned to look at Denise. She was open-mouthed, her eyes wide with apprehension. "My tests came back," I said. "They said I have to come in to get the results. That has to mean it's bad news." My friend looked at me reassuringly. "It'll be all right, David," she said. "I know it will. C'mon! You're invincible."

I don't know how I got through my classes that afternoon. I do recall there were moments I was so involved in discussions with my students that I actually forgot about the doctor. At the end of the day I walked to the parking lot with Denise. We talked about what might be ahead and how I was holding up, things like that. When I got to my car, I turned to her and said, "This is the last time things are going to be normal." If only I could have frozen time.

I slid behind the wheel of my car, turned up the volume on the radio, and headed north on the Palmetto Expressway to pick up my wife. Paula is a history teacher at another high school in Miami. She didn't have a driver's license, so I took her to and from school. This was our routine. As always, she was waiting outside when I got there. She jumped in the passenger seat and I turned down the music and gave her the news.

She tried to be calm, but she was clearly as panicked as I was.

The drive to the doctor's seemed to take forever, but it was too fast for me. I kept thinking that the longer I could put off hearing what he had to say, the longer I could pretend that everything was going to be all right. My mouth was parched dry and my stomach was tied up in knots. Paula tried to make small talk about her day and I was grateful for her effort, but I didn't hear a word. I just kept nodding my head up and down. And trying to catch my breath.

As promised, Dr. Damski was in when we got there. The nurse practitioner pointed us toward his office without making eye contact. The door to the office was open. Dr. Damski was seated behind his desk when Paula and I walked in. His brown hair was cut shorter than the last time I'd seen him and he wore a white lab coat, with a stethoscope around his neck. "Have a seat," he said, pointing to the two tan and brown vinyl chairs facing his desk. He began speaking in medical terms I didn't understand. *Glioblastoma multiforme?* I couldn't even say it, much less understand what it meant. "Okay," Dr. Damski said, "let me show you."

Behind him a large computer monitor displayed an ominous-looking image. To me, it looked like a Rorschach test, a big, gushy, swirling black, white, and gray mash. The doctor turned toward the monitor and pointed. "That's your brain," he said, matter-of-factly. I repositioned my chair to see better, and Paula got up and stood behind me. I had no idea what I was looking at. He pointed to a white mass on a gray background. To me, it looked like something you'd see on the weather report—a hurricane cloud on a Doppler radar screen. The hurricane in my head was a tumor, he said. That was plain enough, but I had a million questions. The teacher in me took over.

"So what does that mean?" I asked. "Is it benign?" Nice try.

Dr. Damski put down his clipboard and pen and looked me straight in the eye. He shifted uncomfortably in his chair. "No tumor in the brain is benign," he said.

"Is it cancerous?"

"Yes, it's cancer."

He might as well have slugged me in the solar plexus. No air. I felt defeated. Hollow. Seeing the terror on my face, the doctor tried to soften the blow he had just struck. "But we don't know too much yet, David," he said. "We need to have a biopsy done." A biopsy for what? He'd already said it was cancer. "We need more information," Dr. Damski said. "We want to know how fast it's growing. Or maybe it's been sitting there for twenty years and growing very slowly."

Okay, I thought. *I can handle a biopsy.* I didn't know then that it meant removing a portion of my skull.

"Can it wait until summer vacation?" I asked.

He pursed his lips, the way I sometimes did when one

of my students asked a question that seemed particularly naive.

"No, that's too far away," he said.

"Okay. How about waiting until Christmas vacation? That's only a month away."

"I honestly don't know if you'll make it that long," he said.

I jerked away from him as if I'd been slapped. And the blows just kept coming. Without treatment, I had a life expectancy of about two months, Dr. Damski said. I looked around his office. The walls were painted the color of hospital scrubs, only more muted, and the art was a poster of a spinal cord and brain. A stainless steel examining table draped with crisp, white paper sat in the corner. It was all so cold and clinical. Shouldn't you at least be in a comfortable setting when someone tells you you're going to die? "How long can I keep being me?" I asked. I already knew the answer. That time had passed.

Paula was stoic, but I fell apart. I excused myself and walked outside to the parking lot to call my brother. Jacques was eight years older, a freelance editor and journalist. Even with his hectic schedule, he had always been there for me. Jacques was my rock. When I heard his voice, I broke down. I could barely choke out my words. *Brain cancer. Terminal. Only months to live.* I was thirty-four years old, damn it. I loved my job. I loved my wife. I loved my life. It may sound like a cliché, but when you're given a death sentence, you really do think to yourself, *How can this be happening? When will I awaken from this terrible nightmare?*

And that's what I said to Jacques between sobs. How can this be happening? I've tried to be a good person. I've tried to do things right. Did I bump my head? Did I eat something wrong? "David," he said finally, "you've got to be tougher than this." That was my brother. Chin up. Tough through it. Be brave. I wanted to be that for Jacques. For Paula. For my students. I didn't want to seem weak, powerless, out of control. I took a deep breath, and another, and then out of nowhere, words I'd never expected came tumbling out of my mouth.

"Don't worry, I've got this," I said. And even stranger than hearing the words was knowing that I did.

2

After a good, soaking cry, Paula and I drove to my parents'
house on Thanksgiving Day. What a difference a fatal diagnosis makes. Before that, I couldn't wait for Thanksgiving. It
was my favorite holiday and the only one where Mom pulled
out all the stops, breaking out her good silver and fine china
and even the crystal stemware that dinged when you tapped
it. All of my immediate family would be there—Mom and
Dad, Jacques and his wife, Tal, and their boys, Emanuel and
Noah, and my oldest brother, Maurice, his wife, Michelle,
and their sons, Jacques and Zach (a girl hasn't been born in
the family for more than thirty years)—as well as extended
family. We typically had anywhere between twenty and
thirty-five people. It took long folding tables that stretched
from the dining room into the living room to accommodate
everyone. It was always the best time. People would start

showing up around five o'clock, and Jacques and I would play bartender while everyone sat around catching up before dinner. The main event would take place around seven and always featured a turkey the size of a Prius and all the trimmings.

The drive from Miami to my parents' home in Pembroke Pines, a pastel-colored subdivision, was around forty minutes. Paula had her learner's permit, and even though she would usually do anything to avoid getting behind the wheel, this time she offered to drive and I was happy she did. I had already decided that I would be strong when I told my parents about the cancer, but I was dreading the conversation and trying to prepare myself. I knew Mom would break down, and the last thing I wanted was to ruin what was for her the most special day of the year.

Jacques and his family were already there when Paula and I arrived. They had flown in from New York a couple of hours earlier. We were all sitting around the living room and I decided it was as good a time as any to break the news to my parents. It was still hours before the other guests would arrive, so everyone would have a chance to recover. Hyperaware of my body language, I was trying to will myself into conveying self-confidence: *Lean back. Cross your legs. Don't fold your arms. Look relaxed.* My parents were seated on the love seat across from me. (They were about to celebrate forty-seven years of marriage and they still sat close together.)

"Well," I said, sounding as casual as if I were about to give the local weather report, "I got the results of the MRI from Dr. Damski."

Mom's face froze.

Tal, sensing something serious was coming, or maybe because Jacques had already told her, got up to round up the boys and bring them into the conversation. At first I worried that at eleven and eight years old they were too young to hear what I had to say. At the same time, having my nephews there made me even more motivated to keep my cool and be reassuring.

"So? So what did he *say*?" Mom asked.

Seeing the fear in her eyes, I wanted to cry. But that would have defeated my purpose. Instead I parroted what the doctor had told me, using the same medical jargon that I hadn't understood but later found on Wikipedia: "Glioblastoma multiforme is the most common and most aggressive malignant primary brain tumors affecting humans, involving glial cells and accounting for 52% of all functional tissue brain tumor cases and 20% of all intracranial tumors. GBM is rare, with incidence of 2–3 cases per 100,000. Treatment can involve chemotherapy, radiation, and surgery." I left out the last part: "Median survival with treatment is 15 months. Median survival without treatment is 4½ months."

My mother burst into tears—the kind of tears reserved for incapacitating grief. It frightened me, and my heart was breaking for her. "Mom," I said, reassuringly, "I really love you, but you need to calm down. I'm going to be fine. Everything is going to be okay."

"What does all this mean?" she asked, choking out her words between howls. I looked at Paula, who was sitting next to me, hoping maybe she had an answer, but she said nothing. So I decided to demonstrate what was wrong with me, just as the doctor had done. Holding my fists together, I said, "This is the size of your brain." I opened my right hand. "This hand represents my healthy brain, which is being crushed against the skull by this growing tumor," I said, holding up my right fist. At that point, my eleven-year-old nephew Emanuel spoke up. "How did you get this?" he asked. *Good question*, I thought. "I don't know," I said honestly. "It just happens to some people. It's very rare, and most people who get it tend to be infants or really old people. Actually, it's a really good thing that someone like me got it. I'm healthy in every other way and strong and I have every chance of beating this." I sounded convincing even to myself.

My father is an artist and very sensitive, and he expresses himself beautifully with paint but usually comes up short when it comes to conveying his feelings in words. His way of handling the news was denial. "Okay," he said finally, with characteristic brevity. "You can handle this. You're going to be okay." Mission accomplished. Dad changed the subject to one of his friends who was suffering from epilepsy (and how at least I didn't have something like that!), and we went about making small talk like the family we were before the word *cancer* raided our lives.

Later, when everyone else arrived, aunts and uncles and cousins and old family friends, I tried to act like the old David. Carefree. Always up for a good time. As far as I knew, no one else had heard about my illness and that would make it easier to try to forget about it for the day. But I was wrong. While Jacques and I mixed drinks and poured wine, my cousin Danny sauntered over to me. "I heard you're sick," he said. I caught my breath, then fell right into the role I had rehearsed for my parents. "Oh, yeah, well, they're taking a look at something in my head," I said, trying my best to sound breezy. "Do you have cancer?" he asked. I sighed and tried to stay casual. "At this point there hasn't even been a biopsy. We don't know anything yet." Yes, I was blowing him off, but Danny wasn't having it. "What kind of cancer is it?" he asked. I had spent the night before studying the paperwork the doctor had given me, and now I recited it back to Danny in terms that were way too technical for him to understand, just as I hadn't been able to comprehend it at first. "I have glioblastoma multiforme," I said. "It's forty-three millimeters in diameter." Danny stared at me blankly, so I tried again. "It's a tumor in my right temporal lobe about the size of a golf ball," I explained.

"How do you feel?" he asked.

I don't know what it was that allowed me to lapse into a moment of abandon, but everything I'd been bottling up came spilling out. I described the painful tingling sensations I'd been feeling along the entire left side of my body and the seizures that left me sick and tired. "It happens at least five times a day," I said, "and it feels like an electrical shock each time." I looked at him again, and this time, I saw tears in his eyes. "I'm so sorry," he said. "That's terrible. I'm so very sorry." He said it over and over again. I said I was sorry, too. I was sorry that I had let down my guard and ruined his Thanksgiving.

At that moment, I made a mental note to myself: *Self, I said, don't do that again! Telling the truth about your cancer is a miserable thing to do to people. What people need to hear is something that will let them off the hook. They can't do anything about it anyway. From now on, tell them, "I'm fine!" That way, they'll feel like, "Good! He's fine!"*

Seeing my cousin's reaction, I realized that if I told people too much about my health, they would withdraw and refrain from sharing their own problems with me for fear of being a burden. That was the last thing I wanted. I knew that cancer would change me, but I would not allow it to rob me of the qualities I valued most in myself, and top among them were optimism and empathy. I was always someone who encouraged and helped others—and the last to pity myself or ask for help.

So began the role I would perform for the next six years.

How are you?

Can't complain! I'm fine! And how are you?

It was a role I would grow into and ultimately come to believe.

I insisted on driving home from my parents' house that night. It would turn out to be one of the last times I drove my beloved Mustang before we turned it in for something more sensible—a thing that looked to me like an oversized toaster but felt safe enough for Paula to drive. For thirteen years, I had driven her everywhere: to the grocery store, to doctors' appointments, for every pair of shoes she owned. Now she was talking about getting her driver's license. The irony didn't escape me. She realized that I wasn't reliable enough to depend on anymore. I'd probably be dead before she learned how to parallel park.

I pulled into our driveway around midnight. Paula went right to bed, but I couldn't sleep and decided to get up and prepare my lesson plan for the following Monday. I sat down at my desk, and panic rocked me like a lightning bolt. *My students!* I thought. *I'll have to take time off for the biopsy. I never take a day off school. They'll want to know where I am. What in the world will I tell them? What on earth can I say?*

That weekend, I spent every waking hour preparing my talk and practicing it until it felt right. I wrote and rewrote notes to myself and talked to myself in the mirror to make sure my facial expressions matched the message I wanted to convey. By midnight on Sunday, I was all practiced out.

3

I was ready, right down to the way I walked into the classroom. My stride had to be just right. Confident and under control. Over the weekend, when I'd been practicing my "I have brain cancer" spiel, I'd decided I needed a prop, more for my kids than for me. I thought it would distract them from the stinging truth of my diagnosis. Teenagers are sensitive (understatement, I know), and for a lot of my students, this would be their first association with disease and I needed to do it right. I had to address my illness but in a way that wouldn't frighten or alienate them. (I was amazed to learn how many people think cancer is contagious.) My cancer wasn't something that could be kept secret—after all, I knew what was ahead, should I be lucky enough to have an "ahead"—and the effects of surgeries, chemotherapy, and radiation were sure to give it away.

Besides, I never kept things from my kids. I was a fierce advocate of the truth, even when the truth was scary or had consequences. Over the years, I'd witnessed the benefits of openness in the classroom and how it gave students a sense of liberation they couldn't have if they were living inauthentic lives. Every semester, after one of our regular discussions about honesty and being true to oneself, a boy or girl always "came out" to the class, and I'd never seen it backfire. I'd watched kids confess to cutting or burning themselves and a number of other personal and painful truths. I knew how difficult that was for them and how brave they were for doing it, and I'd seen how it changed their lives when I and their peers accepted them for the totality of who they were. I saw those students flourish once the burden of their secret was lifted, and they and their classmates learned a valuable life lesson: with trust comes respect. I needed my students to know that I trusted them enough to share life's most sacrosanct passage. Death. I just had to do it in a way that would make them feel safe. *Practice what you teach,* I told myself. *Your kids deserve to know this. They'll have to go through it with you. Make it okay for them.* I figured a stuffed penguin wearing a hat that looked more like dreadlocks might lend some levity to my confession. I don't know where the penguin came from; it must have been a gift from a student. I was just happy I came across it at home that weekend. I named the penguin Winslow. The name just came to me.

Monday. What a glorious day it was, an aqua-colored Miami postcard. I strode into my first-period class with a smile on my face and Winslow in my arms. "Good morning!" I said. "How's everyone today?" I pulled the stool from behind my desk and sat Winslow on top of it. I stood a bit behind the stool to Winslow's right. "I've got something to tell you," I said. "Now scoot your desks in closer." The kids were snickering and looking at each other like I'd finally gone loco. "Okay, what's going on?" they asked. "What game are you playing now, Menasche?" I chuckled along with them.

When everyone was settled into place, I looked at Winslow and started speaking. "I told you I haven't been feeling well," I said, sounding bright. Winslow nodded his head yes. "Remember I had that tingling in my ear?" I asked. "Well, the good news is there's nothing wrong with my ear!" I sucked in my gut and continued. "But I had more tests and they showed I have a brain tumor." I looked up at the class. My kids, who had only a moment ago been laughing and hamming it up, were somber and quiet. "What is a tumor?" someone asked. "A tumor is a growth," I said. The sudden silence in the room was disorienting. My classroom was always buzzing with the excited sounds of learning and sharing. Another student spoke up. "My uncle had cancer and he died," she said, and burst into tears. "Are you going to die?" another asked. "Someday," I said. "Not right now."

I could see how hard they were taking the news. I thought of my cousin Danny and knew I had to recover fast. "Hey," I said. "There's no reason to get upset. I have a great life! Everyone has their bag of hammers to carry and this is mine." I put Winslow aside and launched into a pep talk about how I wasn't going anywhere, and oh no, they couldn't get rid of me that easily.

And then I repeated my new mantra.

"Don't worry," I said. "I've got this."

I was in that class. I was sitting in the front row. I always did. Mr. Menasche walked in with Winslow. I didn't understand exactly what was going on at first. But then he started talking. He started out sounding like he was going to tell us a story, the way he always started class. But then I heard the word "cancer." I was in shock. I started crying. I thought he wouldn't be around the next day. I felt so helpless and alone. Bad for myself, but bad for the students who would never have a chance to have him.

He was one of those once-in-a-lifetime teachers. The ones who teach you lessons you remember long after you leave the classroom. He treated us with respect, and we respected him so much. I mean, c'mon, he told us we could write notes to each other in class. He said, "I'm an English teacher! Why wouldn't I encourage you to read and write?" But his lessons were so absorbing you didn't even think about writing notes to your friends. You just wanted to take it all in, to be a part of it, to learn.

I couldn't bear the idea of him being gone. Or even worse, of him suffering for years to come. I didn't know what to say or what to do. All I could do is cry. Then he said something I'll never forget. "Don't worry. I've got this." I was never so proud of anyone in my life. My heart was full when I left class. And I was smiling.

—*Gyzelle Rodriguez,*
Coral Reef Senior High School,
Class of 2008

4

As the novelist Alice Sebold once wrote, "Sometimes the dreams that come true are the dreams you never even knew you had." I was made to be a teacher. I just didn't know it until I was halfway through college. I backed into my dream come true while I was studying journalism at Eugene Lang College at the New School for Social Research in Greenwich Village. The New School was named by the *Princeton Review* as the best college in the country for encouraging debate and discussion. It was right up my alley. I was a smart-alecky kid who had inherited a love of books from his bookstore-owning parents. The only thing I loved more than a good argument was words. I thought maybe I'd pursue a career in writing. But a plan is only as good as your last experience, and it wasn't too far into the curriculum that I figured I might be on the wrong career path. I was trying out for a summer internship at *Spin* magazine, at the time one of the hippest music publications around, and the editors assigned me a stack of new CDs to review by the following morning. I listened to each of the CDs, then sat at my typewriter and froze. How did I dare criticize the work of the Red Hot Chili Peppers, one of my favorite bands? What if I was wrong? What if the band called to complain? I wrote in fits and starts (mostly fits), staying up all night to complete the review. That morning, when I turned in the assignment, sleep-deprived, my shoulders aching from hours of being up around my ears, I thought to myself, *Are you sure this is what you want?* The answer was a resounding *No way! With this kind of stress, I won't live past twenty-one.*

I got the internship. Other students in the program would have sold their first car to intern for *Spin*, but I wasn't feeling it. *How am I going to do this?* I wondered. *I'm not a deadline kind of guy. I'm going to get permanent writer's block. I'll have a nervous breakdown. I'll never sleep again!* Ever the optimist, I thought of a quote from one of my favorite writers, Jack Kerouac, in the book *On the Road.* "But why think about that when all the golden lands ahead of you and all kinds of unforeseen events wait lurking to surprise you and make you glad you're alive to see?" The unforeseen event lurking in my immediate future was that I didn't have enough money to pay for the following semester, nor did my parents, so I had to give up the internship. I can't say I minded.

Enter the dream come true that I never saw coming. After that skipped semester, and months of working double time busing tables in the city so that I'd have enough cash to pay my tuition, I returned to the New School to resume my studies. About halfway into the semester, one of my favorite professors convinced me to sign up for the Teachers and Writers Program. The program placed aspiring writers in New York public schools for a week and gave them the opportunity to teach while they were there. I was sent to teach a group of eager first-graders in upstate New York. The small village school with its frozen pond in the center was enchanting to a Miami kid like me. On the very first day, I decided that I wasn't going to teach the kids by the book. Instead, I read to them from Walt Whitman's *Leaves of Grass* ("I sit and look out upon all the sorrows of the world, and upon all oppression and shame . . ."). I couldn't help but be animated and energetic when I read it, as Whitman had always had that effect on me.

I looked out at my six-year-old students, sitting Indian-style in front of me, and I saw wonder in their eyes. Their hands shot up before I was finished reading. They wanted to ask questions. "Just wait until I'm finished and we'll talk about it, okay?" I asked. "Okay!" they cried in unison. At the end of the reading, all hands shot up again. I answered some of the questions, then had an idea. "Tell you what," I said, "why don't we just go outside and write our own poems." The kids squealed with delight. I bundled them up and marched them outside like a flock of ducklings. Giving each one a small stack of yellow Post-it notes and three crayons, I asked them to write down the things they noticed—one item per piece of paper. The kids ran around looking at everything, and like Whitman, I thought, had a blissful enthusiasm for their surroundings. They wrote words like "rock," "leaf," "footprint," and "snowflake."

After I noticed one of my little duckies with frozen snot on her upper lip and two others shivering, I shepherded everyone back inside and asked the kids to stick their notes up on the board and rearrange them until they were in an order that the kids liked. When all was said and done, they had written a poem! The students jumped up and down with the same sense of accomplishment and joy that I felt watching them learn. That was it. There was no turning back. That was the moment I knew I wanted to be a teacher.

The dream I never knew I had was about to come true.

He didn't just teach me what to learn. He taught me how to learn and how to love doing it.

—Adrianna Angulo,
Coral Reef Senior High School,
Class of 2008

5

I met Paula while I was at the New School. We were in a philosophy class together. She looked the part of the all-American girl, with dirty-blond hair, translucent skin, and the saddest bluish-green eyes I'd ever seen—except with a twist: the nose ring and the black leather jacket she wore with the name of an alternative rock band, Sonic Youth, spray-painted on the back. Paula was the smartest person in the class, and the smartest person I'd ever met. For me, brains are a turn-on—Oh! The irony!—and she had one big brain. (That brain would later take her to an impressive run on the game show *Jeopardy!*) Anyway, she was always piping up in class with something profound to say and I was intrigued by her intellect (and her jacket).

I remember the first time I realized that I wanted to get to know her outside the classroom. We were in our seminar class, all ten or twelve of us sitting around a round table, and the professor began a discussion about the Greek philosopher Plato's "Allegory of the Cave," from his work *The Republic*. The story, written as a fictional dialogue between Plato's teacher Socrates and Plato's brother Glaucon, is a complex and layered metaphor contrasting the way in which we perceive and believe in reality. (No fluff in philosophy.) The piece was a reading assignment, and we were forewarned to be prepared to discuss it in class. But when the professor asked for input, it was immediately clear from everyone's superficial answers that no one had done their reading. No one except for Paula. She hadn't just read it. She'd studied, dissected, and analyzed it and come to class armed with compelling questions and arguments. It was obvious that reading wasn't enough for her. She really wanted to understand Plato's theory. For me, that was it. I was completely smitten.

When class ended that day, I got up my nerve and marched up to Paula to ask her out. I told her that a few of us were going to the East Village to the 7B Bar (named after the corner it's on). "I'd really like it if you'd join us," I said. I was surprised and excited when, without hesitation, she accepted. It turned out to be a great night of listening to music and spirited discussions fueled by endless bottles of Rolling Rock. We sat at my favorite table by a large window overlooking Seventh Street. Paula was across from me. Toward the end of the evening, my friend Greg leaned in to me and whispered that I should "hook up" with her. She heard him and smiled. I took that as a good sign, that she must have liked me, at least a little.

We all left the 7B in a happy mood, and I offered to walk Paula back to her dorm room in Loeb Hall on Twelfth Street. Neither of us wanted the evening to end, so we stopped in Union Square Park along the way. Paula was a history buff, even back then, and we strolled around the park admiring the statues of George Washington, Abraham Lincoln, and the Marquis de Lafayette. We had our first kiss beside the James Fountain. Paula mentioned that her roommate didn't like having visitors, so I suggested we continue talking at my place. My roommates, Colin and Charlie, didn't object to guests. Lucky for me, Paula accepted my invitation and, after that night, decided to stick around. It wasn't long afterward that we moved in together. I proudly called her my girl nerd.

Paula had also participated in the Teachers and Writers Program and had been transformed by the experience just like me. After two more semesters at the New School, we decided to transfer together to a school with a teacher certification program. We chose a college in Miami, my hometown. For the first month, we lived with my parents, and then we moved to our own place in North Miami Beach. It was a big adjustment for Paula. Miami was a culture shock. She'd been there with me a couple of times—once during Andrew, the category-five hurricane—but those were just short visits. Paula was from Vermont, where everything's green, people are spread out, and there's virtually no crime. Now we were living in a cramped apartment in an asphalt jungle in a neighborhood where the sound of gunshots in the middle of the night was the norm. It was all we could afford.

Once we enrolled in Florida International University, there was no time for fretting about our surroundings. Between waiting tables and school, we were hardly ever home. The teaching program was rigorous and we were high achievers. It was an exciting time. We still had that sense of idealism that so many people lose once they get out into "the real world." I was determined not to lose it. After two semesters, we were on the homestretch. All that was left to do after that was an internship. But first I had a painful lesson to learn: a foot belongs on the floor, not in your mouth.

The last class I needed to take was called Classroom Management Skills, which was basically meant to teach us how to discipline students. Paula was in the same class. The professor and I were as compatible as witches and water. She was a true disciplinarian who believed that teachers must exert unwavering power and authority over their classes to keep them in line. "You shouldn't smile in front of your kids until Christmas," she told us one day. "If you start off nice, you'll never gain control." What? Okay, so I was still a student, but I couldn't imagine such a harsh technique being very effective—it sure wasn't working with me—and I said so. I didn't have much of a filter back then, so you can imagine how that went. I'd probably call my side of the conversation more of an attitude than an opinion.

Needless to say, the professor was incensed. "What do you think, that you can just make everybody love you all the time?" she snarled. I instantly recognized the Machiavellian argument within her words. Machiavelli told his protégé, the Prince, that he could never control others' love. Whether or not they loved him would always be up to his people, but he could decide whether or not they feared him. I didn't want to be that kind of teacher. "No," I said. "But I do think that I can get them to respect me. They'll respect me for being prepared and knowing my material, they'll respect me for caring and trying my best, and if they respect me, then hopefully they'll like me."

I heard a few of my fellow students clapping in response, but before I could congratulate myself on my powerful speech, the applause quickly died down and I heard the professor's chair push back to the wall. She looked at me, with eyes so cold I half expected them to turn from brown to blue, and pointed to the door. "Get out!" she said. *Good job, Menasche*, I said to myself as I lugged my sorry ass out of her classroom. That class was the only thing standing between me and my completing my internship, graduating, and getting a teaching job, and my final grade was "Expelled!"

Lesson learned: always agree with the teacher. (Just kidding.)

With no place to go but into a panic, I sought out one of my other professors, Dr. Gail Gregg, who was also the department head of the College of English Education. Dr. Gregg thought I had great potential, so she took pity on me and found a way around my dilemma. Her solution was to allow me to take an independent study with her. The topic she chose for me was ambitious. My assignment for the semester was to create a full reading curriculum for at-risk kids. I felt so indebted to Dr. Gregg that I poured myself into the project and earned an A. I thanked her profusely, but she answered that thanks weren't necessary. "Just go and be a good teacher," she said. I never forgot it. Paula, meanwhile, stayed on in the other professor's class and we think she paid for my indiscretion with a C. It was the only C she had ever gotten and she never let me forget it.

Dr. Gregg was also in charge of internships, and when it came time for Paula and me to be assigned to a school, she placed us together at Coral Gables Senior High School, me in the English program, Paula in social studies. Then, a few days in, my mentor for the senior English class had a terrible tragedy in her family—her daughter committed suicide—and she didn't feel able to return to school. I was on my own.

The kids knew I had no power over them. But from that first day, I spoke to them as my equals, explaining honestly and sympathetically what their teacher was going through.

"I'm sorry that you guys are stuck with me," I told them. "I don't know what I can possibly teach you, but I promise to try my hardest."

The class had been reading *The Kitchen God's Wife* by Amy Tan, which I had to admit I'd never read. "How are you enjoying the book?" I asked. I got a couple of shrugs, some rolling of the eyes, and at least one yawn in response. *This isn't good*, I thought. I looked ahead on the syllabus and saw that Chaucer's *Canterbury Tales* was up next. "I liked these when I read them in high school," I said. "What do you say we put Amy Tan aside and move on to Chaucer? If any of you want to finish the book, I'll give you extra credit." Eyes lit up. I even saw some smiles. "I haven't read *The Canterbury Tales* since high school, so be merciful with me," I said, "and I'll give you the best I've got."

I went home that night and not only reread *The Canterbury Tales* from cover to cover but learned all the students' names. I'd given them my word and I wanted to show them that I respected them enough to keep it. I wanted to earn their respect and prove to myself that my teaching instincts were sound—despite what the professor who'd expelled me had said. The next day's class was a different game. The students, who had seemed distant and dismissive a day earlier, were discussing Chaucer and asking me questions about writing and literature and even about myself. I knew I had a lot to learn, but that day I understood that the best kind of power at my disposal as a teacher was not the kind inherent to the profession but the power my students chose to give me.

I didn't want my internship to end. I had grown fond of my students and reveled in their accomplishments. And I had to find a job! As it turned out, the job found me. When the school year was over, another English teacher, who was leaving to become a department head at a brand-new magnet school that was scheduled to open in the fall, asked me to join her. Paula landed a full-time job teaching history at Miami Coral Park Senior High School and, at the ripe old age of twenty-four, I signed on for my destiny.

A place called Coral Reef Senior High.

Mr. Menasche's classroom was a place where I felt safe to express my opinions and my views about the world around me. "You're not children, so I will not treat you like children." That was one of the first things he ever said to my class. I just loved how he didn't expect us to give him respect just because he was the teacher. His students have and always will respect him because of the respect, love, and generosity that he showed us.

When you have that sort of connection and admiration for your teacher, it inspires you to always do your best work.

—Jerel Tyrone,
Coral Reef Senior High School,
Class of 2010

6

The morning before my first class, I rummaged around in my closet, looking for something that would make me look teacherly. It was slim pickings. Probably the last time I'd shopped for clothes was at a souvenir stand at a rock concert. Paula tried to help. "These?" I asked, holding up my best pair of Levi's. (Hey, they were clean.) "Mm, no," she said. I dragged out a shirt with a paisley pattern I'd probably had since high school. "This?" I asked. Paula shook her head. "Uh-uh." I settled on a pair of tan khakis, a long-sleeved, army-green button-down shirt (it had been recently ironed), and my brown Doc Martens. Something was missing. A tie. I only owned one. I'd worn it for my part-time job as a waiter at Steak and Ale during college. There it was. Beige and green geometric print, still an acceptable width, not too skinny. I'd picked it up from a vendor on Fourteenth Street in the East Village and haggled the guy down from five dollars to three. It wasn't a perfect match, but it was close enough. Paula helped me tie the knot and I was ready to go. I checked myself out in the mirror. "I'm a teacher!" I said out loud. I could hardly wait to get to school.

A couple of weeks earlier, I'd gone in to check out my classroom. It was gorgeous—fresh paint, shiny new desks, and floor-to-ceiling windows looking out over a lush green courtyard with palm trees and picnic tables painted with the school colors of teal, silver, and black. I hung up a couple of Shakespeare posters and decided that I'd ask my students to do the rest of the decorating. That would help them to feel it was *their* classroom.

I'd also gotten to meet many of my colleagues at around that time, at a retreat at a restaurant called the Rusty Pelican on Biscayne Bay. It was a beautiful late-summer night and at one point I looked across the bay at the Hard Rock Cafe where for the last few months I'd been waiting tables to be able to make the rent. I'd given up my shift at the Hard Rock that night to attend the retreat. As I looked out across the water, it occurred to me that I would have been doing roll-ups (rolling silverware in napkins) about then, except that it was the eve of my dream job. I was about to be a teacher.

I was the youngest person among my new colleagues. Meeting my fellow teachers, I thought, *Wow, they're all grown up.* I had a moment of epiphany just then. I was now a grown-up, too. Teachers from all over had applied to open the new school. We were considered "the dream team," Miami's best. I may have been only in my early twenties, but somehow someone had considered me worthy of the honor.

I was really feeling my oats when one of my new colleagues pranced up to me and briskly introduced herself. "Wow," she said, slowly looking me up and down, from my thick, dark mane of hair to the mismatched laces on my shoes, "you're a rookie."

I thought about that as I dressed for my first day of class, and I decided that to age myself, I'd wear a tie every day and grow facial hair, too. I needed to look the part to feel like I fit in with my peers. *Fake it until you make it,* I told myself.

But as much as I wanted to make a good impression on my coworkers, what mattered to me most were the kids. I couldn't wait to meet them. "The mediocre teacher tells. The good teacher explains. The superior teacher demonstrates. The great teacher inspires," the author and scholar William Arthur Ward wrote.

I wanted to be a great teacher. The best they'd ever had.

———————

I was in his first-period English class on the very first day Coral Reef Senior High School opened its doors, his very first class. From that first class, I could tell that my experience in his classroom was going to be special. He had this approachability about him. He wasn't a lecturer. He was a storyteller. He knew how to teach by sharing his own life experiences. We had a conversation. Sitting at my desk in his classroom, I felt as if the only thing that mattered was those few hours where we were submerged in the world of literature, poetry, and vocabulary.

We read poems from E. E. Cummings, Walt Whitman, and Tupac Shakur. Yes, I said Tupac Shakur. He taught us "The Rose That Grew from Concrete." ("Long live the rose that grew from concrete when no one else even cared.") That was really eye-opening because I realized there was poetry everywhere and in each of us.

I look back and realize he was a rookie, but we never felt like we were in the presence of a teacher who was feeling his way. From that very first day, he had a way of making the most complex things accessible to every student.

Sometimes I wonder if he ever really knew just how much he empowered us, academically and personally. He didn't just teach us, he inspired us.

—Ayxa Barbel,
Coral Reef Senior High School,
Class of 2001

7

I got to class early to put some finishing touches on my classroom. I wanted to liven up the neutral beige walls, to make the room look inviting, so I'd brought books from home to place on the built-in bookshelves, and a homemade collage of some of my favorite American authors to hang behind my desk. I had spent hours putting together the collection of pictures—Walt Whitman, Louisa May Alcott, Emily Dickinson, Frederick Douglass, James Baldwin, Harriet Beecher Stowe, Edgar Allan Poe (glowering), and, of course, Ernest Hemingway. After I nailed the last tack in the poster, I ran downstairs to the principal's office for our inaugural staff meeting. Everyone was chattering excitedly with the anticipation of opening a new school, one that attracted some of the best and brightest students in the state of Florida. I looked around and thought, *This is the best day of my life!*

At the end of the meeting we were handed printouts with the names of our students, one sheet for each class. As I made my way down the long, narrow hall, back to my classroom, my heels clicking on the polished linoleum floor, I leafed through the pages and was overtaken by a sense of awe. My stomach fluttered with butterflies. My students, whom I had imagined and anticipated the way an expectant parent might wonder about their unborn children, now had names. *These are my kids!* I said to myself.

Back in the classroom, I scrawled my own name in big, black letters on the whiteboard. "Welcome to Honors English! David Joel Menasche." With less than an hour to showtime, I practiced my opening act.

"Good morning, everyone! Welcome to Coral Reef Senior High. My name is Menasche. Da-VEED. Joel. Menasche. [Think Sean Connery playing James Bond.] I know it's a strange name. Even though it looks like 'David,' it's pronounced Da-VEED. My father is from Cairo in Egypt and my mother was born in Siberia. The name David is pronounced Da-VEED everywhere except in English-speaking countries. For instance, the Renaissance sculpture *David* by the Italian artist Michelangelo is pronounced Da-VEED."

It was only years later, last summer, in fact, during the planning of a family cruise to Cozumel in Mexico, that I learned that my assumption about the pronunciation of my name—the name my mother had called me my whole life and my whole family calls me to this day—was based on a myth I had apparently created myself as a kid. We were sitting around the dining room table at my parents' house, going over last-minute details of the trip, checking passports. "Why am I named Da-VEED?" Everyone at the table burst out laughing, including my mom. "What?" I asked, looking around the table at my family. My brother Maurice, between fits of hysterical laughter, explained that because he was eleven years old at the time of my birth and the oldest child, my parents had allowed him to name me and he'd chosen the name David after the actor David Cassidy from his favorite TV show, *The Partridge Family*. When my mom said the name with her accent, it came out sounding like Da-VEED. So when I was old enough to say it, I pronounced it her way. Da-VEED. The name stuck and the whole family called me that. Nearly forty years later, after correcting everyone who had ever called me David, and giving my introductory classroom pronunciation lesson probably hundreds of times, I discovered there was nothing at all romantic about my name. I couldn't claim company with Michelangelo's masterpiece. I had been named after David Cassidy from *The Partridge Family*.

8

The first student ever to walk into my class was drunk. (And to think, a few minutes earlier my biggest worry was finding a marker for the whiteboard.) I had just finished practicing my little speech when the kid stumbled in. "How you doin'?" he asked, making his way to a front-row desk and plunking himself down. The boy had long, greasy hair and was wearing a black Ozzy Osbourne concert tee over wide-legged jeans, his wallet dangling from a chain connected to a belt loop, and a spiked metal bracelet on his wrist. As he passed in front of me, the smell of alcohol almost knocked me down. I was bewildered at first. It was first period, a time in the morning when many people haven't yet had their first cup of coffee. I was looking at a fifteen-year-old who was inebriated and it wasn't even eight a.m. And why on earth would he sit right next to me? I would have expected he'd slink to the back of the class. *Nope, Menasche, you're not making this up*, I said to myself. *The kid is wasted. Happy first day of your dream job.*

I walked up to the boy and introduced myself. "Hi," I said. "My name is Menasche. Yours?" (I'd always introduced myself that way, and many of my students picked up on it and called me by my last name.)

"My name is Aaron Rawcliffe," he said, glassy-eyed and grinning. "Nice to meet you."

"Likewise," I said. "You reek of alcohol. Have you been drinking?"

When I looked into the boy's face, I saw some aspects of myself at his age. It hadn't been that long ago that I was a moody, defiant, reckless teenager, taking risks, breaking rules, rebelling against my parents and every other authority figure I could find. I was plenty rebellious when I was fifteen. I was heavy into the hard-core punk skate scene and I dressed the part. My jeans were always torn and I shaved my head bald except for a swath over my left eye and a thin braid down my back. My father nagged me so much about my hair that my mom finally stepped in and asked me what it would take for me to get a normal haircut. "A tattoo!" I said.

What a tough age that was. I was a boy growing into a man's body. My hormones were in space. I was wild one minute and brooding the next, misunderstood and in desperate need of attention. What better way to get it than a punk hairdo and a tat? (Or coming to class drunk.) I figured I had as much chance of Mom's saying yes to the tattoo as I did snagging Danielle Greenberg, the most popular girl in my high school. But guess what? Mom told me to get in the car and we headed to the tattoo parlor downtown. The whole ride she kept asking if there wasn't something else I wanted instead. "An aquarium maybe?" she asked, knowing how much I loved fish. I thought about it for a minute but decided a tattoo would impress my friends a lot more than a couple of fish in a big bowl. "Nah," I said. "But thanks anyway."

We got to the tattoo parlor, and while I was wandering around, looking at all the flash art on the walls, I heard moaning behind me. I spun around and saw a big, burly biker dude getting a tattoo on his neck. His chest was covered in blood and ink and he looked like he was in agony. I turned to my mom, eyes wide. "How many fish did you say I could get for the aquarium?"

My parents were still in for a couple of years of angst until, right after high school graduation, I packed my bags and went to live with my brother Jacques. Jacques was twenty-five and living a bohemian lifestyle in New York. His world was figuratively and culturally foreign to the prosaic existence we'd lived growing up in southern Florida. He and his three roommates lived above a dry cleaner in Brooklyn. I'd come from a housing development in a landscape of straight lines, wide-open highways, and manicured lawns, to live in a railroad flat with books and records strewn everywhere and skyscrapers blocking the sun. I loved living in a hothouse of budding artists, where people played in bands and painted on canvas and read philosophy for pleasure. Jacques and his friends worked lowly jobs in bookstores to be able to pay the rent, but they were young and passionate and intellectually engaged. I loved being there.

I got a job waiting tables at a restaurant called Nadine's in the West Village to pay my way. (A little side story: When the restaurant was reviewed, the writer referred to me, the busboy, as "a tender little morsel that I would like to wrap up and put in my back pocket," which my oldest brother, Maurice, gleefully brought to my attention. Sure, I was pretty cute, but "tender little morsel"? I figured if I could survive that, I could survive pretty much anything.)

Jacques had expectations of me, and he was clearly in charge, but he treated me with respect and I didn't want to do anything that would disappoint him. He was my best teacher. He introduced me to some of my favorite books, from *On the Road* to *A Confederacy of Dunces*, and inspired my love of writing and literature. My parents put in an A-worthy effort, but it was my brother who guided me away from my self-destructive teenage behavior by teaching me how to embrace education and learning.

I wanted to be that same kind of anchor for my students.

I asked the kid a second time. "Have you been drinking, Aaron?"

"Well, um, yeah," he said.

"Listen," I said. "If some square-ass English teacher like me can figure out you're drunk, how do you think you'll ever fool the cops or the principal? I'm sorry you're doing this to yourself, but don't come to my class like this again."

I had never gotten drunk before school. My school had allowed us to leave campus for lunch, and there were times when I'd go with my friends who had cars, drink, and then go home and sleep it off. But this thing with Aaron, it was dark-thirty and the kid was already drunk. What party is going on that early? I was really concerned. It was my first day on the job and I didn't know what to do, so all I could do was follow my instincts, and my instincts told me that sending the kid to the principal or writing him up would only alienate him more. I wanted to establish a relationship with him and keep a close eye on him. He needed someone to be there for him.

That night, after school, I went home and devised a two-part plan. I knew Aaron was begging for attention, so I would give him a lot of positive attention, but only when he deserved it. Kids know when you're being authentic as opposed to coddling them. If he said something provocative during a class discussion, or wrote a particularly good essay, I'd praise him. If I liked a concert T-shirt he was wearing, I'd tell him it was cool. The second part of the plan was to make sure my class was worthy of his undivided attention.

If I was going to accomplish something in this job, I would have to think out of the box and come up with ways to help the students want to learn what I was teaching. The measure of my success as a teacher wasn't how much I was being paid, or even having the kids learn every lesson, but having them recognize how hard I was trying so that they would try equally hard. I had high expectations for my kids, but no higher than the expectations I had for myself.

And as the saying goes, "Students float to the mark you set."

From that day on, I would set the mark high. For them. And for me.

_____

I don't know what I was thinking. For some crazy reason I decided I wanted to sit right next to the teacher. I walk in, the first one there, and I'm real cocky, like "I'm here for school!" He walks up to me, he's real calm, and he asks me if I've been drinking. I say, "Uh, um, I dunno, what do you mean?"

Of course, I had been drinking. I'd chugged two 32-ounce malt liquors right before I got there. I didn't want to be in a magnet school. I wanted to go to regular public school with all of my friends, but my mom bribed me with tickets to OzzFest if I agreed to give it a try. My friends offered to drop me off at my new school before they headed to public school. But on the way, they decided to cut classes, pick up some beer, and go to the beach. I said, "Are you crazy? It's the first day. I've got to go to school." My buddies had fake ID, so we stopped at a 7-Eleven about a half mile from my school and bought the beer. They got me two 32-ounce bottles of Mickey's Ice Malt Liquor and I downed both of them. Then I went to class.

I looked up at him and he didn't look mad. He looked . . . confused. That threw me. Other teachers would have been like, "What the hell is wrong with you? How dare you come to my class like this?" I would have been sent to the principal and suspended, maybe even expelled. He didn't do that. He looked at me with this really sincere look of concern. He wasn't pulling the "authority figure" thing with me. He was showing me that he cared and he was treating me with respect.

I never came to class drunk again, and I never missed Menasche's class. I ditched classes all the time, but never his. I knew he had high expectations of me and I didn't want to disappoint him because he was working so hard to help me succeed.

—Aaron Rawcliffe,
Coral Reef Senior High School,
Class of 2000

9

Having settled into our teaching careers, Paula and I decided to buy our first house. We couldn't afford to stay in South Miami where our apartment was, certainly not on teachers' salaries—we were each earning less than forty thousand dollars at the time—so we spiraled outward until we found a house tucked on a residential street between two six-lane roads in the flight path of Miami International Airport. The ranch-style starter home was thirteen hundred square feet with two bedrooms and a bathroom with no window, but Paula and I fell in love with it. Of course, the Realtor had only taken us there in daylight, and it was only after we moved in that we realized the house shook every time a plane took off or landed, and the motels nearby were hourly and catered to the prostitutes that prowled the streets by night. Never mind. We were young and in love with each other and with the idea of having our own home, so we made the best of it.

On weekends, we decorated with hand-me-down furniture from my brother Maurice, Paula's family pictures, and modern art from one of my students who painted in oils. My mother always had houseplants, so we filled the house with pots of Boston fern and weeping fig. When I stood on the front lawn, I was Ben Cartwright on his eighth-of-an-acre Ponderosa in the middle of Miami. I planted a tree and announced to Paula, "I'm going to watch this grow until it reaches the sky!" It was our little postage stamp of paradise, and we'd sit at our kitchen table in the mornings, drinking coffee and smiling at our good fortune. We had each other and now we had officially put down roots by owning our very own little piece of real estate.

All that was missing was a couple of kids.

Paula and I had been going back and forth about having children. She finally convinced me that maybe we should start with a dog, which was a happy compromise. I'd wanted a dog my whole life, so on a Saturday afternoon shortly after we moved in, we drove to the local pound and adopted our first child—a mixed-breed puppy no bigger than a football with paws the size of a bear. We named him Milo. By the time he was six months old, he was eighty-five pounds of energy and exuberance and growing fast. When my parents came to see the house for the first time, Milo got so excited that he leapt through the screen on the living room window, bounded across the front porch, and tackled my mom (in a friendly way). She was terrified of him after that.

With Paula and Milo and a house with a fenced-in yard, I felt as if I had achieved another dream. I had my own family. The perfect family, as far as I was concerned. But what does every perfect family want? What else? Another perfect family member. And once Milo had grown into his paws and was officially bigger than me, we adopted a sister for him. Lucy was half bulldog and half English boxer. She was small but sturdy and she could hold her own with Milo. They soon became the best of friends. Three stray cats later, we were the Brady Bunch of SW Fourth Street. I called our home Menasche Manor.

10

Over time, the walls of my classroom became papered with my students' artwork: a brightly colored abstract named *Esmeralda* for the gypsy protagonist in Victor Hugo's *The Hunchback of Notre-Dame*, a mobile with the characters from *Huckleberry Finn*, and, later, a portrait of my brain painted in oils from the MRI image. The corkboard on the wall next to my desk became covered with the students' school photographs, eventually hundreds of them, and my bookshelves were jam-packed with their favorite books and inspired essays from classes past that I didn't have the heart to throw away. Sometimes, room 211 felt more like home to me than home did. I lived, ate, and breathed teaching. I got to school early, left late, and worked well into the night trying to come up with fresh ways to get my kids to want to learn. Their input—about what they responded to, and what was relevant to their lives—was my homework. By observing them, learning about them, and, most important, listening to what they had to say, I tried to develop new ways of teaching.

One of the first things I did with a class was ask each student to stand and tell me about their best teacher and worst teacher, and their reasons for picking each. That exercise alone showed me that *how* you teach is the key to getting students interested. What I discovered during those very revealing dialogues was that students want you to have a combination of qualities that aren't always compatible or easy to achieve. The teacher my students wanted was concerned and thoughtful but not so nice as to be seen as a pushover. They wanted someone who cared but not a pal. You had to speak loudly enough that they didn't strain to hear you, or they'd lose interest. Soft-spoken was equated with dull and dull earned you a big, red F. The kids wanted a teacher who respected them, but they didn't need to feel equal in all ways. They understood you were there because you had more experiences and accomplishments than they did, and that was cool, just don't talk down to them, please. That was a big one. They didn't want to be patronized. Nor did they want to be bamboozled. I can't tell you how many times I got to the middle of an essay and found that the student had embedded a snarky note that said something like "I'll bet you're not reading this!" I always circled it and scribbled, "I'll bet you're reading *this*!" The truth is, I pored over each of my students' essays for hours and wrote so many comments with my red pen that the paper looked like a crime scene. If they were going to put in the time writing, I was going to put in the time reading and helping them make it better.

I discovered that kids want a teacher who's demanding and expects a lot from them. Expectation was a great motivator. By the end of my first year, I'd tossed aside dry textbooks and given my students a reading list of twenty-five books to choose from. I called it the "major works assignment" and included, among others, *The Great Gatsby*, *Animal Farm*, and *The Bell Jar*. Along with the list, I gave the kids a synopsis of each book and told them to pick one they thought sounded interesting and read it whenever they felt like it. If they didn't like the book they chose, they could switch, but they had to read a book and create a project about it by a certain deadline.

In class, we covered titles ranging from *The Hunger Games* to my favorite novel, *A Clockwork Orange*. We covered the exalted—Steinbeck and Hemingway and Faulkner, and Dickinson and Whitman and Frost. But I also taught using song lyrics from rappers and poetry by people like the Harlem Renaissance writer Gwendolyn Brooks *("We real cool. We / Left school. We / Lurk late. We / Strike straight . . .").*

You have to come up with some pretty good stuff to distract teenagers from the drama of their lives—the broken hearts, and friendship triangles, and boyfriend problems and girlfriend problems, and oh, those painful breakups! Kids are self-centered. If it's not about them, or they're not somehow involved in the subject matter, they're not real interested. One assignment was to create a pictorial autobiography. The students had to come up with ten quintessential events from their lives. They were asked to write a simple sentence for each of the events, no adjectives or adverbs (I learned to ride a bike), illustrate it with images, drawings, photographs, and put it all together in a collage. The results were stunning, and sometimes hilarious. "I learned to swim" was matched with a picture of a swimmer chased by sharks. "I learned to drive" was accompanied by a magazine cutout of a couple of crash test dummies in a crushed car. The students loved it. Then, just when they thought they were done, I asked, "Have you guys heard the expression 'A picture says a thousand words'?" They nodded. "Good," I said. "Look at your collage and tell the story in a thousand words. Or at least enough words to fill the front and back of the page."

I often recommended Kerouac's *On the Road* to my students for their final essays. The story is based on the travels of Kerouac and a friend, and their search for self. It's not for everyone: my student Massi Gonzales, a chatty girl with a flair for the dramatic, was quite adamant that it wasn't for her. "This book doesn't make any sense!" she said, flying into my classroom after school one day. I shrugged. "Then switch books," I said. I suggested she try Tom Robbins's *Still Life with Woodpecker.* An offbeat love story, it's set in a pack of Camel cigarettes (it's complicated) and you either love it or hate it. "Okay," she said, rolling her eyes.

Massi came to class the next day, her eyes wild. "What is wrong with you?" she cried. "This book doesn't make any sense, either!" No way was I going to let her off the hook for the project. "Keep reading. Find a way to have fun with it." That she did. When the day came to present her final, Massi arrived early. When it was her turn to make her presentation, she stood in front of her classmates and acted out scenes from books and mimed her tortured attempts to read them. Her performance was as brilliant as her idea. With a little encouragement, she had taken what she saw as a mind-numbing assignment and turned it into a masterpiece. I left school that day with a little bit extra pep in my step.

Class time often turned into an animated discussion. I worked hard to have the assignments inspire creativity, even if it was in a nontraditional way. My approach was meant to help my students empathize, and in turn to respect the authors and characters they encountered, with the ultimate goal of their respecting other people in their lives. When preparing to teach an essay called "The Ways We Lie" by Stephanie Ericsson, I started that day's class by asking the kids to write in their journals about a time when they either told a lie or were lied to. That was an eye-opener for everyone, including me. One student wrote about being a little girl who deeply believed in Santa Claus, but then one Christmas Eve she discovered her father wrapping presents and realized her parents had lied to her. When we discussed her essay in class, she said she never really trusted her father after that. It wasn't so bad finding out there wasn't a Santa Claus, she said, but learning her parents had betrayed her was traumatic. "Who do you trust if you can't trust your own parents?" she asked.

The exercise turned into a broader discussion over grades of lies and how even the seemingly most innocent of them provoked ripple effects. As Ericsson wrote in her essay, "We lie. We all do. We exaggerate, we minimize, we avoid confrontation, we spare people's feelings, we conveniently forget, we keep secrets, we justify lying to the big-guy institutions. Like most people, I indulge in small falsehoods and still think of myself as an honest person. Sure I lie, but it doesn't hurt anything. Or does it?" I thought it was a great question and I tossed it out to my students. I asked them to categorize their lies as either white or bald-faced. The white lie evoked the most interesting debates. Everyone knew a big lie was wrong. But what about a well-intentioned lie? ("Yes, Virginia, there is a Santa Claus!") At first, most of the kids defended it but then saw that the sweet little lie had huge implications for their classmate, who admitted that her trust issues created tensions in her relationships with her friends and her boyfriend.

I'd give the kids an example of a harmless little lie, what

we called fibs when I was growing up. For instance, "Your girlfriend asks you how she looks and you tell her you think she looks great. But you're lying. Is that okay?" The collective response was almost always the same: "What else would you do? Why would you want to hurt her feelings?" At which point, I'd introduce the words of great literary minds on the subject. One time it would be George Bernard Shaw's, "The liar's punishment is not in the least that he is not believed, but that he cannot believe anyone else." The next time I'd use John Steinbeck's passage from the book *East of Eden*: "Most liars are tripped up either because they forget what they have told or because the lie is suddenly faced with an incontrovertible truth." Another one that really got the kids thinking was from Rhodes scholar and lexicographer Bergen Evans: "A man who won't lie to a woman has very little consideration for her feelings." (Meaning, of course, that he fears the woman can't handle the truth.) Those provocative discussions inevitably led students to conclude that most lies are told from fear and, taking it a step further, that the lies we tell are an admission of how fearful we really are. That was quite an epiphany for them.

Throughout the year I was pushed to understand new ideas about the world and how people viewed themselves in it. I learned how to read the words behind the words, to listen to the voices of authors through their syntax and word choice. The

magic of language was visible to me and I learned how to har-
ness and play with it.

And then he taught us about the real world. Through him,
I came to understand that a life well lived is in the pursuit
and the sharing of knowledge. If we can properly understand
the world, then maybe it is not our obligation to affect it today
but to help the next generation, to give them the tools to create
change, to inspire a better world.

—*Alberto Herrera,*
Coral Reef Senior High School,
Class of 2009

I remember vividly the first assignment he had us do. We were
to type up (double-spaced of course) what exactly we wanted
to do with our lives, all of our hopes and dreams for the future
and how we would go about achieving them. Once the assign-
ment was turned in, he met with us individually to discuss
what we'd written. Holding my paper in his hand, he said,
"Vicky, this is not your voice. What you wrote is all a bunch
of bull and I don't buy it. What is it you really want to say?"
This question hit me like a ton of bricks. I was dumbfounded.
What seventeen-year-old truly knows what she wants when
she can't even decide what college she wants to apply to? But
something happened. From that point on, I finally stopped try-
ing to do things for the sake of getting a good grade or pleasing

a teacher and really started to think about what I wanted out of my education and, most importantly, my life. I never had a teacher give me such a profound gift. But that's Menasche. He doesn't try to push anything on you, or try to make you think a certain way, or accept some fluffy bullshit answer to his questions just for the sake of giving you a grade. He is continually asking you to search for truth, whether it's in literature or in life. He tries to make you think outside the box.

—Vicky Campadonico,
Coral Reef Senior High School,
Class of 2009

———————

Eventually, I found that one of the best ways to instigate meaningful discussion was a system I named the spiral. It's pretty clear-cut. I drew a simple spiral on the board and pointed at the center. "How about we start at the beginning?" I asked. "We all start at birth. Originally, you're entirely self-centered. You cry when you're hungry or sleepy or have a dirty diaper because you want these problems to be fixed. You don't care that you're keeping your parents up. You just want to be satisfied."

I moved the marker a little bit farther along the spiral. "Let's say you're three or four years old," I said. "Your mother gives you a lollipop. You love that lollipop. In fact, your whole world consists of this one lollipop, but you drop it, it gets dirty, and then your mother throws it out. You cry and cry and cry because you think you have lost the only thing that matters to you; you have lost *everything*. At this point, you're just starting to concern yourself with things outside of your own being, but you only care about things that immediately affect you."

I continued moving the marker farther around. "Now you're eight years old," I continued, "and you see your mother crying. You want to go over and help, but instead you just walk away and continue about your business. You don't care that much yet, but this is where the seed is planted. Just a few years later, you finally begin to feel and show real emotional responses to others. At the age of ten, when you see Mom crying again, you go over and hug her. As time goes by, we are slowly pushed outside of ourselves and begin to care about things that concern us personally less and less."

Finally, I got to near the end of the spiral. "Many of us never get here," I explained, "but this is the goal. You *want to be here*. Being at this point means you now care about the past, the future, and things that don't directly affect you, for instance, starving children in Africa, the war in the Middle East, or poverty in third-world countries. This is when you can empathize with others and act with true respect and kindness because to be here is to care about others more than you care about yourself."

Amazingly, the spiral went viral at the school. Kids traced spirals on their notebooks and drew them in pen on their skin. Art students drew them in their sketchbooks, music kids on their staves. The spirals could be seen all over campus, on banners and bulletin boards and lockers—a reminder for my students and kids who had never even taken the class to think beyond their own needs and desires.

When I saw how effective the spiral was, I began looking for other ways of integrating life lessons and literature.

That's how I came up with the priority list.

11

One evening after Paula and I finished up dinner, she went into the bedroom to call her mother and I stayed in the living room rereading my copy of Shakespeare's *Othello*. I'd read the play so often over the years that the pages were worn and yellowing, but my students were having a tough time getting into the story and I hoped that by rereading it I might be able to come up with a way to make it relatable to them.

Paula was still on the phone a couple of hours later when I finally had an idea. "I think I've got it!" I said to myself. What if I made a list of words that applied to everyone's life—words like *honor, love, wealth, power, career, respect*—and asked the students to number the words in order of how each of the characters might prioritize their lives. So, for instance, the list for Othello, a Christian Moor and heroic army general, might begin with *honor*; Iago, Othello's ensign, who seeks revenge on him after being passed over for a promotion, would more likely have *career* at the top of his priority list; and Desdemona, loyal to Othello to the death, *love*. My hope was that prioritizing the words would help the students identify the characters' differences, as well as their commonalities, and see that people in general are complicated creatures who are rarely all good or all bad. (Although there isn't much that is redeemable about Iago!)

That morning, for my first class, I wrote the names of the characters on the board and the list of words next to it, then asked the students to copy the lists in their notebooks and rank the priorities for each person in the play. The kids got so into it that, when the bell rang, most of them lingered a few minutes longer, animatedly discussing their lists. I repeated the assignment for all my classes that day, and each time the same thing happened. The students were getting to know the characters and developing connections with them and, at the same time, getting to know themselves. One would say, "I'm like Iago," and another would reply, "I'm more of an Othello," or "I'm loyal like Desdemona."

The exercise was so effective that the following year I expanded the list with words that were more nuanced and harder to qualify—words like *independence*, *spirituality*, and *style*. Then I asked the students to apply it not just to characters in a play but also to themselves. Afterward, I'd invite them to come up to the board and place their ranking next to each word for all to see. That took guts—they were revealing themselves to their peers and trusting their classmates not to judge them—but that simple assignment gave the students flashes of insight into themselves, and it helped them to identify and empathize with each other. What had begun as an exercise in literature had evolved into a life lesson. And the kids loved it.

I learned a lot from their lists, too. Often the way they ordered their words was a clue to a deeper story. For example, if Amy S. put *career* above *education*, she was probably focused on college as a springboard, but Malcolm B., who listed *education* first, probably hadn't decided on a career yet. The placement of the word *love* was always especially revealing. If Nicole F. put the word *love* next to *family*, there was a good chance it represented a future family, a dreamed-about husband and kids she was thinking of having one day. But if Miguel T. put *security* next to *family*, he was probably thinking about his parents and siblings. In short, their lists were a true reflection of what was important in their lives at that moment, or at least what they *thought* was important before they and their classmates dissected the words and discussed what they really meant.

One of the most poignant stories the assignment produced involved a student named Ryan, a painfully shy kid who was easily intimidated by his classmates. Ryan, who had a beautiful voice, was in the chorus and never displayed more emotion than when he sang. When I assigned the priority list exercise in class, he turned beet red. The way he twitched at his desk, trying to figure out the right answers, I could tell he was way out of his comfort zone, and as I walked around the room, glancing at the kids' papers, I looked down at Ryan's list and saw that he ranked *privacy* first, followed by *family*, then *sex*.

A few weeks later Ryan came to me during lunch hour and sat in the red upholstered armchair next to my desk. He fidgeted in the seat, picked at his fingernails, and stared into his lap, but he finally got what was eating him off his chest. "I'm gay," he said. "And I've never told anyone before you." I patted Ryan on the shoulder. "It's okay. I'm proud of you. That took a lot of courage." I could see the tension drain from his body. We continued to talk throughout the semester and I continually encouraged Ryan to trust his family and friends enough to tell them the truth, which he eventually did. It took a while, but his parents finally came around.

Students often confided in me and I took that trust seriously, but I also knew my limitations. If I suspected that one of them was in harm's way or that professional intervention was needed, I made sure that the proper people were notified and the student got the necessary help. But most times the kids just needed to know someone noticed and cared enough to sit and listen. The priority list was a valuable tool that often helped them (and me) to identify what was going on in their lives.

That list wasn't magic, but somehow the ordering of the words did have some weird power to dislodge well-kept secrets and unlock deep, subconscious truths—often before the kids even knew what was happening. Sometimes I'd pick up on something, some clue in their ordering, and share my guesses about what it meant with them. "How could you possibly know that about me?" they'd ask, blinking. "How did you know I was having trouble with my parents?" or "Who told you I was in love?" Their lists revealed more about their lives and what mattered to them than anything they ever said aloud. The priority list helped them see the truth of their to-days and conceive the possibilities of their tomorrows. Soon enough, it would do the same thing for me.

Menasche told us what an important time we were in in our lives and how the decisions we made then would affect us later. He let us feel the weight of the world on our shoulders, but he helped us carry it—writing papers, asking us questions, writing priority lists. He did anything he could to get us to talk, to speak with intention, so that we could learn how to be adults, and so that we might listen to one another, and listen to the people we were becoming with each lesson.

In high school, so many adults make us feel pressured to

decide what to care about, telling us what we should and shouldn't value: friends, grades, money, popularity—an endless tirade of their own ideas and -isms. So few adults ask us to start from scratch, from within ourselves, and dictate our own priorities.

The List forced us to look at ourselves and question what we really valued, but in a way that didn't scare us or pressure us. It was a way to get us to figure ourselves out so we could decide what kind of adults we wanted to be.

—Melissa Rey,
Coral Reef Senior High School,
Class of 2012

————————

I still have one of my lists scribbled on the back of a hall pass you gave me. It was the first one of mine that you read, and I keep it tucked away in one of my sketchbooks, along with some of my most treasured notes and pictures. I even wrote a whole paper for a college English assignment about your priority lists and how they helped me.

—Holly Jean Henderson,
Coral Reef Senior High School,
Class of 2010

12

"Am I dead?" I asked.

A masked figure loomed in the bright lights above me.

"What do *you* think?"

It was the winter of 2006, and the surgeon, Dr. Arias, had just removed a section of the tumor to take some pressure off my brain. He said the "low-grade diffuse glioma" tumor had been growing in my head for years. The bad news was that it wasn't going anywhere and wouldn't get any smaller than it was, which was about the size of a golf ball. The good news, and I considered it to be very good news, was that the surgery hadn't killed me or affected my motor skills. I could still walk and talk—and, even more heartening, if the cancer continued to grow at such a slow rate, I could live a relatively normal life for years to come. If you had to have terminal brain cancer, this was as good as it got.

I couldn't wait for them to wheel me back to my room so I could see Paula and Jacques. They were there, waiting for me—my ever-loyal family—ready to rejoice in the good news. Something else was waiting for me, too, although it took me a minute, through a fog of anesthesia, to figure out exactly what it was. Tied to the foot of my bed was a giant, shiny helium balloon. I didn't know much Spanish, but I could read what it said. *"Es una niña!"* It's a girl! A gift from my oldest brother, Maurice, the balloon was the only one left in the hospital gift shop. "Maybe the tumor was a girl," Jacques quipped. That cracked everybody up, providing some well-needed levity after a harrowing couple of weeks.

After three or four days, I talked the doctor into an early release. There was nothing left to do but change the dressings on my incision, and I could do that at home, I said. So the nurses put a turban of bandages on my head, wheeled me to the exit, and sent me on my way.

The following Monday, I was back at work. The kids had just returned from winter break. I felt nauseous and woozy, but the only obvious sign that my brain had been invaded was the shaved patch of hair over my right ear revealing a horseshoe-shaped scar laced with black stitches. Would it sound strange if I said that was one of the happiest days of my life? I was exactly where I wanted to be and with the people I wanted to be with. The sun was shining, my students were clamoring to see me, and I was back in the classroom. I had a disease that I could live with. For how long? The doctors were vague in their answers but basically said they didn't know. So much depended on whether the tumor behaved itself and didn't start acting up. Okay. I could live without knowing when my life would end. Didn't everyone have to do that?

For the rest of that year and the next, I lived. Just lived. I never missed a day of school. I accepted the roles of adviser to the National Honor Society and coach of the school roller hockey team. I went with Paula to garage sales and picked up cheap baubles and kitschy trinkets, mostly for the fun of talking the seller down on the price. We still went to hockey games and the beach, and to watch bands play at the local club, Churchill's.

Then one day in 2009, I got a headache. I was in school, preparing for our first open house of the year, a chance for parents to come to meet teachers and review their kids' class schedules, and it was mandatory that we be there. No excuse was good enough for missing it. Certainly not a nuisance headache.

But my head hurt all day, and the pain seemed to get progressively worse until, by the time the open house began, I could barely see straight. I told myself that it was because I'd been at school for twelve hours already and hadn't eaten any dinner—there hadn't been time to run home in between—but this wasn't your ordinary stress or hunger headache. The only way to describe it is *excruciating*. But I had to stay. "Get it together, Menasche," I said when I heard the footsteps of the first parents coming down the hall toward my classroom.

When my room was full, I began my usual "welcome" speech. "Welcome to my worst nightmare. I've been here since before seven a.m. and now I have to make a great impression on my students' parents!" As always, the icebreaker worked and everyone chuckled. *Only ten minutes more and you can go home,* I told myself, going onto autopilot.

A ten-minute eternity. Endless parent questions. Grades. Extra credit. College. I stuck it out until the last of them left the room. Then my knees buckled and I collapsed. Not an "Oh, I'm so exhausted" collapse, but involuntary. I mean I literally keeled over.

A few minutes later, Denise stopped by my classroom to see how it had gone and found me slumped over my desk. By then, I was coming to, but my head felt like someone was taking a sledgehammer to my brain. *Boom! Boom! Boom!*

Denise called Paula, and I met her at Dr. Damski's office. He looked worried, then bolted into action. Looking me over, he immediately called an ambulance to take me to Baptist Hospital, a mile away. Dr. Damski followed it there. Within moments of arriving, he had the results of my new MRI in his hands. I was in trouble, he said. Serious trouble. So serious, my life was in imminent danger. If I didn't have brain surgery right then, I would die.

While one nurse helped me onto a gurney, another one wrote a note with my name and Social Security number and taped it to my chest. With Paula at my side, an attendant raced me past the admittance desk and into an elevator, pressing the button for the second floor. "Call Jacques," I whispered to Paula as the elevator doors slid shut. Dr. Damski was already waiting in the OR. As the anesthesiologist pricked my skin and I felt myself starting to drift away, I wondered if I would ever see the face of my wife or my brother again.

The surgery took several hours and, by the time it was over, Jacques was there. He had been in California, interviewing people for a documentary film he was making, and caught the first flight to Miami. The doctor said that what he had seen on the MRI was the alarming image of my tumor, which had grown to the size of a baseball. My passive tumor had suddenly turned aggressive and was pressing so hard on the midline of my brain that it was killing me. If he hadn't rushed me into surgery and resected it to minimize the pressure, I would have died within hours. In fact, he said, the parents of my students were lucky I hadn't dropped dead introducing myself at the open house.

Only six months had passed since I had posted on my new Facebook page: "David Menasche just got back from his six-month checkup at Duke University and is in totally stable condition. Sweet."

Indeed it was.

Now I posted a picture of myself, postsurgery, with an update: "The pathology report is in. I have a level 4 (the highest level) gioblastoma (the worst kind of tumor) at its most aggressive level. I need immediate radiation and chemotherapy. Six weeks, every day. OK. So you know, the median life expectancy with this kind of treatment is 12 to 15 months."

Within minutes of the post, dozens of people responded with sweet words of support and encouragement. But it was a tongue-lashing posted by one of my students that got my attention. Heather Marie Wilson, a spunky kid who had graduated from Coral Reef the year before, read my post and heard the undertones of self-pity. "So, all week everyone has been saying to me, 'Heather, go on Facebook and look at Mr. Menasche's page. Go quick. It's sad,'" she wrote. "And now, I finally found the time to check (here it is, 2:30 am) and I'm sincerely pissed. At you, at them, at the situation. It's quite obvious that these people don't know who they're dealing with, and quite frankly, I feel as though you've lost sight of that, too. I remember the first time you came out and told our class Jr. year about your illness. You made us cry, worrying about you, scrambling to find things to do to help you, to ease your pain, to NOT lose you. I remember I was at my desk CRYING! And you looked me dead in the eyes and told me not to worry. That you weren't going anywhere! It honestly pains me to see you like this, and to see people get sorrowful over this. Honey, you're here! And you're going to be here for a while. You're too much of a damn fighter to just give up now. Anyways, I have an 8 o'clock class to prepare for. I expect by tomorrow I'll see a brighter status."

Out of the mouths of babes. I couldn't help but smile when I read it.

———————

The first time I ever walked into his classroom, he wasn't there yet. I was kind of nervous because I'd heard about his cancer. By then, he'd had it for a couple of years and everyone knew about it. So he walks in with this swagger and I see this huge, gnarly scar on the side of his head. It was scary-looking. He drops onto a stool and looks out at the class with this great big smile and he says, "Good morning, ladies and gentlemen! My name is David Menasche and, yes, I have brain cancer." Just like that. Then he moved on to tell us how much we were going to love his class and how much he expected from us.

—Jennifer Brewer,
Coral Reef Senior High School,
Class of 2009

13

I'm not always a quick study, but I learned real fast that having someone tell you how long you're going to live—or, rather, how long you aren't—changes your priorities in a hurry. Mine became survival. For the next two and a half years, I sat for countless doctors visits, doing everything they said I should to try to keep the cancer at bay. After school became a routine of grueling chemotherapy and radiation treatments. It took a toll on my marriage. The treatments left me chronically nauseous and fatigued, not to mention bloated, and bald on the right side of my head. I lost whole swaths of my early memories. The simplest things—how I got the scar on my left knee, for instance—were a mystery to me. Family trips to Disney World and what had apparently been my favorite blue Schwinn bicycle existed only in pictures. It was frustrating, to say the least. My first fifteen years were pretty much gone, but my family and friends were kind enough to help me fill in the blanks with stories and images. The more cancer pilfered my brain, the more responsibility Paula had to take on to keep us afloat. We were slowly reversing roles, and her newfound independence and my neediness caused friction between us.

My seizures also intensified. The antiseizure medications the doctor prescribed had a terrible effect. I'm a passionate guy, but when I took the meds, I couldn't feel extremes—not real anger or sadness or happiness, nothing. It was as if the edges of my emotions had been shaved off. One night, for instance, I was watching a comedy on TV with Paula, a funny movie called *Teachers* (of course) starring Nick Nolte and Ralph Macchio. In one scene, a teacher seemingly engrossed in an open newspaper sits at the desk behind a neat pile of handouts. When the bell rings, the students file in, take the handouts, and go to their desks. The teacher never looks up, and at the end of the class period, the students file out again, dropping the handouts in the same spot, without ever realizing their teacher is dead. As we watched, Paula was in hysterics. I recognized some of the lines as being funny, yet my response was flat. I couldn't laugh.

Because I love having fun, joking, smiling, *feeling*, I went off the meds and put up with the seizures. I actually got good at them. I could tell when one was coming on. That gave me time to pull to the side of the road if I was driving or excuse myself from the classroom if I was at school. Usually I just told the kids I needed to go see another teacher about something, then stood in the hallway for a few minutes until the symptoms passed.

———————

It was easy for me to forget he was sick, of course, until it wasn't. One day, during my senior year, I took a little detour to pay him a visit in his classroom. He was teaching a full six-period schedule and I knew the work was wearing him out. When I walked into his room, there were several students around him, each waiting a turn for his attention to ask some question on an essay they were rewriting. He seemed so pleased to see me, excitedly waving me over. He was always happy to see me, even on a bad day. Even if he didn't really have time for me, he would act like he did and listen anyway. Sometimes I went to his classroom just to see if I could help. This was one of those times.

"Can I do something?" I asked.

He led me a few feet away from the other students, and because I knew him so well by then, I could tell something was wrong. "I need you to take care of them for me," he said.

I was a bit confused. "What?" I asked.

"Answer their questions," he said. "See what they need."

"Oh, right. Sure." Such a simple task, I thought sarcastically.

He must have sensed my confusion because he quickly

said, "I'm having a seizure," and then walked briskly out the door.

I did what he asked and went to each of his students to see if I could answer their questions. A minute or so passed and he returned. For the first time, I saw him for who he really was: a very sick man. His mouth was slightly open on the right side and he wiped away spittle with his sleeve. He smiled at me and resumed his class. I returned after school, only to catch him on his way out. He brushed me off when I asked about the earlier incident. "It was nothing," he said. Then he started talking about exams, which were only a few weeks away. Of course, he wasn't going to let illness get in the way of his students' growth.

—*Melissa Rey,*
Coral Reef Senior High School,
Class of 2011

———————

I think the worst part of the whole treatment thing was the MRIs. My brain was photographed more than Lady Gaga. Doctors' orders were that I go for the procedure every two months, so they could regularly monitor the tumor for activity. I'd go to the clinic, give blood, and then lie down on a table that slid into a narrow tube that came to about three inches above my nose. If that doesn't make you claustrophobic, nothing will. For two hours and nine minutes (I always wondered, *Why the nine minutes?*) I had to lie perfectly still in that cylinder while the machine clanked loudly about its business. I couldn't hear myself think, and I couldn't clear my throat or scratch an itch because even that kind of tiny movement meant they'd have to start the procedure all over again.

I dreaded the MRI. My first time in the machine, they injected me with a radioactive fluid about halfway through the procedure and I instantly threw up. The vomit burned my throat, went up my nose, and ran into my ears and eyes as I lay there trying not to move. Cancer sucks. But lying in a tube unable to move with puke running down your face sucks, too.

It got to a point where I was living by those tests. They showed whatever minuscule changes were occurring in my brain. The best I could hope was for the tumor to remain static. Any change was bad change, so I'd spend the following two months in a state of dread, wondering if I'd be granted another two when the results came in. Every time a nurse called to say, "The tumor is stable," I'd do a little happy dance.

I know the doctors thought it was the treatment that was keeping me alive, but I knew better. My job got me through each day. My students were my life force, my breath, the blood running through my veins. In school, I wasn't sick. I was teaching. The only way to beat cancer was to not let it stop me from doing what I loved.

I continued to immerse myself completely in being a teacher, relishing each moment I still had with my kids. I celebrated their accomplishments and pushed them twice as hard when I knew they could take it. Our time was precious, and I had to make it count. I was determined that we continue to bond over learning and a deep appreciation and respect for each other, and not my cancer. A classroom is a place of discovery, and we taught each other about the importance of the written word and self-expression. But it was also a place where we practiced humanity and cultivated healthy personal relationships. I felt a deep need to affect those around me while I still could, and to form new memories to fill the void left by my old ones.

Without even knowing it, by sharing those precious moments with me, by helping me to make those memories meaningful, my students gave me the will to live.

14

One night, after finishing a round of chemo, I was sitting alone on my couch at home, flipping through the channels on the TV, wishing for someone to talk to. Paula was on the phone with her mother again, and I knew she'd be a while. I don't know how the urge came about or why at that particular moment, but I grabbed a sheet of lined paper and one of my favorite roller ball pens and starting writing down what was important. My priority list. It was the first time I'd taken the time to do it and I was excited to see how it would turn out. But when I finished writing and read it over, my heart sank. For my number one priority I put friendship, followed by education, independence, and respect. I hadn't listed either marriage or love as one of my top priorities. I stared at the page in disbelief, bewildered by my own candor. Hearing Paula's laughter coming from the bedroom, I began to think about what *her* list would look like. I knew family would be at the top; her mother and sisters were the most important people in her life. I was pretty sure that after that she'd say career, education, and pets, in that order. (Our dogs, Milo and Lucy, and cats, Zoe, Norah, and Betty, were her surrogate children.) Where did I fit on the list?

For the last couple of years, I had seen cracks forming in our relationship. Rather than bringing us closer together, cancer was the interloper that had come between us. Or maybe we had been growing apart and the disease was the mirror that wouldn't allow us to pretend anymore that we hadn't noticed. As I sat there on the couch by myself, feeling more alone than I ever had in my life, I wondered when our priorities had changed. When had we stopped grading papers together and watching hockey? Or taking in local art shows? Or trolling the neighborhood for garage sales? When had Paula begun spending every evening after dinner on the phone? And when had I begun staying longer at school, and volunteering to be an adviser for extracurricular activities that took me away on so many weekends? When had I last told her I appreciated her? When was the last time we had really kissed?

15

"Idle hands are the devil's tools" is a timeless parental expression, but it wasn't one my mom ever used, as I was a kid who rarely stood still. If I wasn't playing football in the street or jousting on bikes using broom handles as lances, I was skating. Constantly skating, grinding curbs on my scraped-up board until Mom impatiently called me inside for dinner. Fifteen years later, the games had changed, but my energy level hadn't. Call it a work ethic. Call it being a workaholic. Either way, I took it as a compliment.

Still, the 2011–2012 school year was challenging, even by my own standards. I was spending twelve hours a day at school—teaching back-to-back classes, mentoring students, attending faculty meetings, coaching, chaperoning—then I'd go home and grade papers and prepare lesson plans before collapsing into bed. On top of that, there were the treatments, the twice-a-week radioactive injections that beat me down into a nauseous, listless pulp.

All the same, I'd grown accustomed to my new way of life. I dealt with my symptoms as casually as others might handle a runny nose. I'd run to the bathroom, heave into the toilet, flush, brush my teeth, and then fly back to the classroom in just under three minutes. Sure, the effects of the disease and the treatment were a nuisance, but my health was fine. I even won "Teacher of the Year" for my region, beating out thousands of educators throughout southern Florida for the title. I felt as if I could go on living that way forever.

July 10 changed that.

At the time, Paula was in Vermont, visiting her sick mother. That night I went to meet my friend Adrianna at New Wave Billiards on 107th Avenue in Miami. When I arrived, Adrianna was already there. We paid for a rack of balls, grabbed a couple of beers from the bar, and went to claim our table. During the first game, while she was catching me up on her life, I ran the table. The second game was more competitive—Adrianna didn't like losing—but I took it anyway. "How about one more?" I asked, egging her on. Adrianna nodded her head tentatively. "Guess I'm a glutton for punishment," she said.

The jukebox played "Brownsville Girl" by Bob Dylan ("Brownsville girl with your Brownsville curls / Teeth like pearls shining like the moon above") and I geared up, determined to make it three for three. I picked up my cue and chalked the tip for drama à la Paul Newman in *The Hustler*. Examining the table, I found an easy shot, a pigeon that only needed a tap. But as I set up, white spots suddenly danced on the green felt and my arm jerked forward. I watched the ball misfire embarrassingly across the table and ricochet aimlessly off the sides. I figured the spots were a reflection from the overhead light and didn't give them much thought. Adrianna laughed and we moved on. But when I positioned myself for the next shot, I felt fuzzy and off balance—the way you might when you try to walk after getting off a roller coaster.

As I stood there, waiting for my equilibrium to return, the cue fell out of my left hand. I bent over to pick it up and saw the same dancing spots on the floor. I began to get nervous. "Something is wrong," I said, looking at Adrianna. I tried picking up the cue with my left hand but couldn't lift it. "What's going on?" Adrianna asked, concern in her eyes. I was feeling wobbly. "I don't feel well," I said. "I'm going home." Adrianna was right on my heels as I headed for the door. "I'll follow you," she said.

I slid behind the wheel of my car and headed down Eighth Street, the same route I drove every day to take Paula to school. Home was only four miles away. When I got close, I looked in my sideview mirror and changed from the middle to the left lane to make my turn. Then wham! I plowed smack into a tow truck idling beside me. I never saw him. *How in the world could I miss a tow truck?* I wondered. Adrianna pulled to the side of the road while the truck driver and I inspected our vehicles. His truck was okay, but the left side of my car was all chewed up. "I'm so sorry, totally my fault," I said sheepishly. He waved me off. "No problem, man," he said, climbing back up into his vehicle.

With Adrianna still behind me, I drove the couple of blocks home and called Paula at her mom's. I was pretty shaken up as I recounted what had happened. "I looked," I said. "But I didn't see lights. I didn't see anything. You couldn't miss that truck, but I drove right into it."

Paula suggested I make an appointment with an eye doctor, which I did, but I was mad at her for not offering to come right home. The following day, I left the house at around noon. I passed the car in the driveway, which looked much worse in the bright sunlight, and started limping toward the strip mall where the doctor had his office. But where were the pastel-colored houses? The carports? My neighbors? Staring ahead, I didn't see any of that. I realized that suddenly my world had been reduced to the ribbon of sidewalk directly in front of me. Beyond that, nothing.

I briefed the eye doctor on my medical history and told him about the accident. He did something called visual field testing, where you wear a set of goggles and face a bowl-shaped instrument, and then push a button every time you see a flash of light. The results came out in the form of a computer printout. "This is your line of vision," he said, looking alarmed. He pointed to a pie-shaped diagram. The left side of the pie was blank. "That means you didn't see any of the flashes of light on that side," he said. The other side showed more activity. A dark-colored sliver, from twelve o'clock to two o'clock. I'd lost 80 percent of my sight.

I went home feeling defeated, my left arm hanging at my side like a wet noodle, my left foot dragging behind me. The cancer was gaining on me. Time to take it seriously. After weeks of additional tests, my doctors concluded that I'd had a seizure at the pool hall—hence the spots. The seizure had caused my brain to swell and the swelling had instigated immediate and severe neurological damage. In the time it had taken for me to shoot the seven ball, I'd lost most of my vision and about half my strength on my left side.

"Now what?" I asked.

For the next several weeks, I underwent steroid treatments to reduce the swelling of my brain, hoping that somehow the medications would work their magic before classes started in the fall. Although the treatments were worse than the angry messages my tumor was sending, the thought of going back to my class kept me motivated to stick with it. A few weeks later, with little improvement to show for the treatments, I asked my ophthalmologist if there was any hope of regaining my vision. "Well, there's always hope," he said in a noncommittal way, "but you should probably get used to this." The future certainly didn't look very bright. Other doctors concurred: one more episode, they agreed, and I could lose the rest of my sight completely and be left totally paralyzed.

What did this all mean? Blindness? Cancer? Paralysis? I think I tried not to think of it at all. It was incomprehensible. All I knew was that I wanted to get back to work, that my kids needed me, and I needed them. We still had so much to do, and I was ready to go. Hell, I'd even planned for the coming school year, fleshing out lessons that had been effective and dropping those that hadn't worked. In addition to *The Catcher in the Rye* and *One Flew Over the Cuckoo's Nest* and *Siddhartha*, I'd decided I'd add plays for my honors English classes: Arthur Miller's *Death of a Salesman* and Tennessee Williams's *A Streetcar Named Desire*. Maybe the kids could act out some of the scenes. For my advanced placement students, I'd chosen passages from Dave Barry's soon-to-be-released book *Insane City*, which they could relate to because it was set in South Florida, in addition to the standards: "The Gettysburg Address" and Martin Luther King's *Letter from Birmingham Jail*. I'd even picked up new literary posters for my classroom and bought a new pair of Doc Martens to wear on the first day.

Now I just had to get past this setback and through the rest of the summer.

16

That August, I went on a family cruise to Mexico to celebrate my fortieth birthday. The trip had been planned months in advance, but the timing was awful. I was just learning how to tie my shoes, unscrew the cap on the toothpaste, and button my pants using only my right hand. Every day was a reminder of what I couldn't do now. Of who I couldn't be. I wasn't *me* anymore. At least before I could pretend I was the old David by hiding my illness—running off to the bathroom to throw up or pulling on a hat to cover the dent in my head. Now, with my leg dragging behind me and my arm dangling feebly at my side, there was no way to conceal that something was seriously wrong. I think what got me down the most was looking in the mirror. Through the shard of vision I still had left in my right eye, I could only see half my face, and the image staring back at me was unfamiliar and unsettling—bloated and bald.

I had been hoping I'd recover at least some of my sight and mobility before the cruise rolled around. But in the weeks since the seizure, I hadn't seen any improvement, and everything I couldn't do was suddenly magnified on the ship. Being marooned in a strange place with some three thousand people milling around illuminated just how helpless I really was. It had been hard enough navigating a familiar street to walk to the eye doctor. On the ship, I was trying to maneuver passageways so narrow that one person had to step aside for another to pass, and I was always knocking into someone or tripping over unseen objects. The floors were slippery from ocean spray, and with wet passengers moving back and forth between the pool and their cabins, even able-bodied people were losing their footing. For me this was pure hell. I was constantly falling down. For the last six years I had prided myself on being able to disguise my disease by living a life that, at least from the outside, looked pretty normal. Now I was apologizing to complete strangers for being lame and nearly blind.

My poor family. My brother Jacques had started planning the trip the previous spring, months before I was stricken in the pool hall. A family vacation was something my mother had dreamed of for more than twenty years—since the 1980s, when Jacques left home in Miami to live in New York. The last time we'd all taken a trip together was when I was two years old and we jammed into the family station wagon and drove to the Great Smoky Mountains in Tennessee. My fortieth birthday seemed like a perfect excuse to finally make Mom's dream come true, and canceling at the last minute would have broken her heart.

So there we all were—Paula and I, Jacques and his family, Maurice and his new girl, Robin, and my parents—aboard the cruise ship *Imagination* for four glorious days of Las Vegas–style neon and glitz at sea. I could see how much having us all together in one place meant to Mom. She was glowing when the ship pulled out of the Port of Miami. The last thing I wanted was to ruin it for her.

On our first day at sea, I was headed to my cabin when I knocked into a cleaning cart piled high with sheets, towels, and toiletries. I never even saw the thing. It jerked forward, and a pail full of mop water went flying, splashing the floor, walls, and everything on the cart. The guy pushing it grunted something about watching where I was going. I couldn't blame him for being annoyed. I'd just made a lot more work for him. I didn't want him to think it was carelessness on my part, and I quickly apologized. "Hey," I said. "I'm really sorry. I don't see very well." Maybe he nodded or maybe he didn't. I didn't take the time to find out. I spun around and hobbled off, headed who knows where? I was so humiliated I just had to get away.

That was just the beginning of my misadventures. It seemed as if every time I left my cabin, something else happened. When I tried walking down a flight of stairs from the observation deck, I tumbled from the top to the bottom, landing on my knee. I passed a kid in the hallway and accidentally slapped him in the back of the head with my swinging left arm. An older man I presumed to be his father stopped to admonish me. "Hey! What do you think you're doing?" he cried. I could see through the tapered lens of my good eye that the man was incensed. He was a big fellow and the thought crossed my mind: *What if he throws me overboard?* It was an irrational thought, but it frightened me nevertheless. I wouldn't have been fearful before. I'd grown up swimming off the shores of South Florida, and I'd been a lifeguard when I was in high school. But I was hardly that guy anymore. Once again, I found myself apologizing. "I'm so sorry, sir," I said. "I didn't mean it. I don't see well, and my arm is sort of paralyzed." I don't know if he believed me, but he went on his way.

After that, I was afraid to do much of anything. I was constantly on alert, trying not to bump into someone or trip over a deck chair or slip on a wet floor, and I began spending more and more time brooding alone in my cabin. My mom, God love her, tried to get me to make the best of it. Before the cruise, I think my parents were in denial about my illness. It was easy to forget I had a deadly tumor growing in my head because I seemed so normal. Now they could hardly ignore the truth: I was walking into walls and falling down stairs. Every time I looked at my mother I saw the worry in her eyes, but she tried pretending everything was okay. "Da-VEED! Go to the pool!" she'd say. "You love the water!" Or "Go to the casino. It's so much fun!" I couldn't tell her I was afraid of drowning in the pool and worried that the bright lights and loud noise of the slot machines would trigger another seizure.

We were all under a lot of pressure to act joyous and happy for Mom's sake, and that grew old fast. Paula's face was taut with tension and my brother Jacques spent most of the time running around making sure everyone was having a good time. My father, meanwhile, sat by the pool for hours on end. It was easier to pretend there.

At dinner one night, I was aware of Dad watching me struggle with my utensils. I would choose food from the buffet that I could eat with either a fork or a knife, since I couldn't handle both at once. I'd stab a piece of meat with the knife, or roll pasta around the fork, then shove it into my mouth before the food had a chance to fall in my lap. I'm sure it wasn't a pretty sight, and Dad offered to design a combination fork and knife when we returned home from the cruise. It was a sweet gesture, but for me it was yet another reminder of what I could no longer do—something as simple as feeding myself with dignity.

As time wore on, I felt myself spiraling. I tried sleeping, but my mind wouldn't allow it. I was manic from steroids the doctor prescribed to control the swelling on my brain, and negative thoughts churned in my head. I couldn't stop thinking about all I had lost and what, if anything, my future held. *What am I going to do when this is over? Sit at home with a remote in my hand?* I had tried for so long to keep my chin up, and now I was disappointing everyone, including myself, with my morose moods.

One night, after everyone else had gone to bed, I looked at Paula, sleeping beside me, and started thinking about our last cruise together. It was thirteen years earlier, in 1999, when we were married at the foot of the Mendenhall Glacier during an Alaskan cruise. I'd planned the wedding for June 21, the summer solstice, and a day of endless sunlight. It was just me, Paula, a justice of the peace, and a few Inuit witnesses who botched our wedding photos, but it felt perfect to me. Back then, Paula and I were partners in everything. We went to bed and woke up together. We listened to the same music, read the same books, took pleasure in each other's company. I went with her to JCPenney to help her pick a dress for our wedding and had the inside of our wedding bands inscribed "Truly. Madly. Deeply."

It was that way for a long time, but now we were drifting apart.

As I lay there, I tried remembering exactly when things began to change. I knew my illness had taken a toll—on everything from our love life to our finances. We'd been distancing ourselves from each other for a couple of years, but recently we'd begun to feel like strangers. I know one of the reasons we stopped connecting is that Paula saw me differently after my diagnosis, partly because I was now sick, but also because I *was* different. Cancer changed me both emotionally and physically. There was suddenly a scar on my head, titanium screws and plates in my skull, and no hair to hide any of it under. It became difficult for me to care about the future or the past I struggled to remember, so I became obsessed with the present moment and living solely in it. That made me insatiably curious but also impatient and restless. It hurts to say it, but I think Paula simply didn't like the new me. That was never clearer than on the trip to Mexico. She was spending most of the vacation in a deck chair, reading history books for her master's degree. When I'd ask to join her, she'd suggest I come by later, after she got through a few more chapters. When I wanted to go to a certain buffet, she said she wasn't in the mood for that kind of food. We went to bed and woke up at different times. While I stood on the observation deck, looking at the stars, she went to the casino with Maurice. I couldn't blame her for not wanting to be around me. Between my misery over being sick and my erratic behavior fueled by the steroids, I couldn't stand my own company. I had hoped Paula and I could reclaim some of what we'd lost while we were out at sea. Sadly, we seemed to grow even further apart. Our cabin bed was so compact we couldn't help but touch each other, but I knew she no longer felt about me the way she once had. There was no softness left, just the hard edges of a breaking marriage. I knew it was ending.

With my family pretending not to see—and the irony doesn't escape me—I finally managed to hit rock bottom while aboard a Carnival Fun cruise ship.

I had struggled through six years of brutal cancer treatments for the sake of my loved ones—because they didn't want to lose me. But I was never afraid to die. I was afraid of living without a purpose. Now, as I saw it, the cancer had taken everything from me. My well-being. My dignity. My independence. My relationship. And what about my job? *How can I still teach?* I wondered. I couldn't drive anymore. I couldn't see well enough to read. How could I possibly be the teacher that either my students or I had come to expect of me?

In a moment of panic, I turned to my brother Maurice. "What if I lose my job?" I asked.

Maurice turned to me, looking truly puzzled. "Well," he said, "it's not like it's the best job ever."

"But it was," I said. "It *was* the best job ever."

On the last night, I joined Jacques on the balcony outside

his cabin. It was a tiny deck, only big enough for a couple of chairs, and we squeezed together with our backs flush to the sliding glass door and our feet dangling over the railing, sixty feet over the water. Miami was within sight, and while I felt a sense of dread about returning to my life there—whatever that might be—as Jacques and I sat there, under the stars, looking out over the ocean, I felt my mood begin to lift. The sound of the boat moving over the water comforted me. As long as I was moving toward something, I thought, I had something to look forward to. A purpose. A future. We sat there in silence for a long time, listening to the sound of the ship pushing through the current.

Jacques finally spoke up. "What will you do if you don't teach?" he asked, taking a drag of his cigarette.

I'd been thinking about words attributed to the late Tupac Shakur that I'd shared with my students so many times: "You can spend minutes, hours, days, weeks, or even months over-analyzing a situation; trying to put the pieces together, justifying what could've, would've happened . . . or you can just leave the pieces on the floor and move the fuck on."

"What will I do?" I asked.

"Yes," he said. "If you can't teach, what will you do?"

"I think maybe I'll travel," I said.

"Where will you go?" he asked.

"I think I'll go to see my kids," I said.

September 2012

Coral Reef Senior High
To Whom It May Concern
Subject: Mr. Menasche's retirement

Hello,

My name is Jessica Packer, a former Coral Reef Senior High School student, and now a Tufts University graduate. My time at Coral Reef Senior High was some of the best years of my life. The campus, the incredible education I received as both an artist and a regular student, and, of course, the wonderful staff members and teachers. One of the most influential people that I met while at Coral Reef was a teacher, David Menasche.

I met Mr. Menasche in my junior year when he was my AP English teacher. He taught me a lot about English and even more about life. Just to begin with, his teaching skills are remarkable. He was able to easily gain the respect of the entire class just by showing us his personality. Most teachers make the entire class listen either by being a friend—showing their comedic and slack side to try to relate to us—or going the opposite route by being extremely strict to frighten us into being well behaved. Mr. Menasche was different.

He explained to us who he was, how he grew up, and how he came to teach at Coral Reef. He demonstrated he was to be taken seriously by, on the very first day, kicking someone out of class who disrespected him. And most importantly, he got his students passionate about literature by being passionate about it himself. He was a wonderful teacher and friend. If I needed anything— advice, someone to listen, or even some tough love—he was there. He paid close attention to his students, and if one of them seemed a little off, he noticed right away and pulled them aside to check on their well-being. He treated us as adults, giving us responsibilities as well as making us act like adults. It felt good to have someone in a school treat us that way.

Since graduating in 2007, I have kept in touch with Mr. Menasche. I still call him that, out of respect. I still write to him every few months. As you can probably see on his Facebook wall, students from years and years past are constantly writing on his wall telling him how much of an incredible influence he has had on their lives.

The thing that makes him a real inspiration, of course, is his struggle with brain cancer. Through all of the rounds *of chemo, he still came to work and did an incredible job. He blew the lid off of AP English scores—which is something people in perfect health couldn't do. His passion for teaching took precedence over his health. It literally took him becoming legally blind for him to decide to retire. Not chemotherapy, not his hair falling out, not losing weight or fainting, or the nausea. Blindness. That is a very inspiring teacher.*

17

Every day when I woke up, I reached for the phone with my left hand, hoping it would be better and, when it wasn't, wondering if I should make the call. I got my answer when, one morning shortly after I returned from the cruise, my hand was too weak to hold on to the receiver and I was too blind to find it on the floor.

That same day, I called school to say I wouldn't be coming back. *I'm so sorry. We had been hoping you would get better. If anything changes, we'll find a place for you.* A two-minute phone call and, just like that, my life's work, my reason for getting up every day at dark-thirty, was gone. "They say when you are missing someone that they are probably feeling the same, but I don't think it's possible for you to miss me as much as I'm missing you right now," the poet Edna St. Vincent Millay wrote. As I placed the phone down, I already missed the classes I would never teach, the students I would never have. For my whole adult life, teaching was what I loved, what I did, who I was.

After Paula went back to work, I spent my days sitting in our living room, watching a TV I couldn't see. Walking was painful and I was trapped in the house, alone and feeling anxious. My sudden physical dependence on others shattered my self-esteem. Most days, I counted the hours until Paula got home, sort of like a dog waiting to be walked. I wasn't just bent anymore, I was broken. Cancer had taken my memories, my independence, my freedom, my marriage, and now my students. What was left? Trips to the doctor? Treatments that left me chronically nauseous and tired?

I went for my regular checkup and the doctor told me my kidneys were failing, not from the cancer, but from the chemotherapy. There was a new drug he wanted to try, he said, something experimental, which had its own side effects but didn't cause renal failure. "You need to start this now," he said.

I don't know what it was—maybe the condescending way in which he was taking charge of my life—but I felt the old David infiltrate my body.

"No," I said flatly.

The doctor hesitated and looked at me. "You *have* to do this," he said, his voice stern. "You need this." He looked at his watch. My reluctance to simply agree to his new treatment didn't fit into the scheduled consultation time and he was clearly annoyed. *Sorry, pal, but you have more time than I do.*

How do you know what I need? I thought to myself. *You guys have been telling me what I need for six years. It isn't working anymore. I'm crippled and I'm blind.* The traditional plan for cancer patients is to try every line of treatment possible until they're either in remission or dead, and for six years I'd conformed to that standard. But it was no longer for me. Quitting treatments went against what the medical community (and most level heads) believed was best for me, but I needed freedom—physical freedom from needles, IVs, and claustrophobic MRIs, and the intellectual freedom to go against the grain and choose to discontinue those treatments. I'd spent many years teaching my kids to be independent of mind and body; now I needed to be brave enough to follow my own lesson. I could accept that I didn't have any say in my fate. The cancer was going to kill me. But taking drugs to prolong a life of misery was a choice, my choice.

So?

"No," I said again, hearing the conviction in my own voice. "I decide."

The doctor impatiently waved me off—as if to say, *Well, if you choose wrong, you've written your own death sentence.* Perhaps. But for the first time in years, I felt unburdened. Free. I remembered the promise I had made to myself long ago.

Cancer had taken my past and would take my future, but it wouldn't take my present. It was time to make those words mean something.

As I sat there, in that cold office, whatever was left of my life became crystal clear. It was time to live. Really live. I have always believed that someone who has a "why" to live can figure out the "how." For me, that meant returning to my students. I began to think a lot about my conversation with Jacques on the cruise ship. "What will you do if you don't teach?" he had asked. When I talked to him about taking a trip around the country to see my kids, it was more like a pipe dream, the wishful thinking of a dying man. But the more I mulled it over, the more I began to think that it made sense. Why *couldn't* I go? I had overcome challenges before, plenty of times, so what was stopping me now? Cancer wasn't going to write the last chapter of my life. I could still write, thank you. All my best stories were based on my experiences with my kids over the last fifteen years, so why not see as many of them as possible to get the next part of the story: their stories! Why would cancer get in the way of that?

I had never been one to give in to a bully. I went to a rough high school and I frequently felt threatened, knowing that if I went down the wrong corridor, I could get messed with. But that didn't stop me from taking that hallway. Once, I found myself staring down a group of Latin Kings, a violent gang in my school. As I continued walking, they started calling out to me, taunting me. "What are you doing here? You looking for trouble, man?" I'd been through things like this enough times to know that any sign of weakness from me would be taken as an invitation for a thrashing, so I decided to take things in the other direction. I sat down right where I was standing and said, "Move me." It was a challenge to the gang, and it might have been the stupidest thing I've ever done. Before I even had a chance to defend myself, one of them started dragging me along the ground. The whole thing suddenly struck me as so ridiculous that it was funny. I burst into laughter, and the other guys looked at each other. They didn't know what to do with me. One by one, they started laughing, too, and finally the gang member who had been dragging me stopped and sat down on the ground next to me.

"Little brother, what's your name?" he asked.

"David," I said.

"Well, David," he replied, "You are one tough little mother. . . ."

So where was that tough little mother now? How was cancer more threatening than a gang of thugs? Why couldn't I sit down at the feet of my new adversary and demand that it move me?

I decided I would stop all treatment and take the trip. I had found my own cancer cure: be healthy, be happy, and have a sense of purpose. It didn't matter how long it lasted. What mattered was how I spent my time. The plan I was formulating was to travel around this magnificent country, experiencing the places I'd always wanted to see and visiting with people who had so enriched my life over the fifteen years I'd taught, people I loved, who loved me—my students. We didn't need a classroom to learn from each other. I would tell them stories and ask them to tell me theirs. Perhaps I could reclaim some of the memories I'd lost, and I would make new memories. And I wanted to know: had I made a difference in their lives? Then, if I made it back, I would write about my journey so that other people who were facing down adversity—no matter what that was—might be inspired to see that where there is a purpose, there is a life worth living. How you live it is up to you.

"You're crazy," Paula said when I told her. "How can you take a trip when you can't see and you can hardly walk? And what about your treatments?"

"I'm quitting all of my treatments," I said.

"So basically this is a suicide mission."

"No," I said. "I'm making the choice to live while I can."

I figured I had one up on a lot of people: I finally really believed I was going to die. All my doctors had told me so, and I'd read the statistics about my kind of brain tumor. People who got six years were considered lucky. I was going on seven. With its latest punch, the cancer had let me know, in no uncertain terms, that I was living on borrowed time. I finally got it. I was going to die. Most people don't think about death as if it pertains to them. They live life like it's infinite. There's always tomorrow—to reach out to a friend, to call your parents, to say "I love you." I had lived that way even after my initial diagnosis—as if I had a million tomorrows. But when you really know you're going to die, when you're prepared for death, that's when you learn how to live. It's a bittersweet lesson. Just when you learn how to live, you die. But there's so much beauty in it. All of a sudden, the sun in the sky is a reason to rejoice, flowers come alive, a gentle breeze on your face feels almost spiritual. Who you are is defined no longer by what you do but by what you give and how you love. To me, that felt like a good death.

I began telling friends about my vision quest, as I called it, and set a launch date of November. In my head it would be an opportunity to ask my students to teach me as I once taught them, and in practicality I would be asking them to assist me on a journey that would take me over deserts and rivers and miles and miles of open road, to meet new people and see first-hand the America that Kerouac and Whitman wrote about. I'd never traveled farther west than Illinois, but I had former students in places like Arizona, Texas, Oregon, Washington, and California. Maybe I'd even get to fulfill a dream that had long inspired me—taking a swim in the Pacific Ocean.

With my new purpose, my mood changed almost overnight, and as the poison from the treatments drained from my body, I felt healthier than I had in years. I was pretty confident I could get a few people to take me in during my travels, but how would I get the message out to my kids? I'd stayed in contact with many of them over the years, but I'd taught more than three thousand students during my years at the Reef. What would be the best way to try to reach them all? How else? I posted a note on Facebook:

> To my Coral Reef Senior High family: I want to thank you all for our time together. You gave my life pride, purpose, joy, satisfaction, and meaning. It truly has been my honor to have been even a small part of your lives. Before anybody gets weepy-eyed, let me just fill you in on my plan. I'm taking to the road. I plan to hitch, take buses and trains (yes, cane and all), and make my way across the country to the Pacific Ocean. So let me know where you are and if you've got a couch for a night.

Within forty-eight hours I had offers from students in fifty cities.

"You've got a bed in Atlanta!"

"I'm in Charlotte, NC—come anytime!"

"Boston College!"

"I have a spare bed here in Virginia. Would love to have you!"

"Mr. Menasche!!! I am in San Francisco. Let me know when you get here!"

"We'll figure out something in Asheville."

The outpouring from my students of love and offers of a place to stay overwhelmed me. Reading them over that first night was one of the few times since my cancer diagnosis that I broke down. They were tears of gratitude. The kids I had nurtured and cried over and laughed with wanted to give something back to their teacher—as if they hadn't already given me the gift of a beautiful life.

In the weeks that followed, I spent every day going through offers of shelter, contacting my potential hosts, plotting routes, and making travel plans. My friend Heidi Goldstein started a fund-raising page to help me pay for the trip. The planning was arduous but was finally getting my blood moving. I could feel myself waking up. Clearing the fog. I bought a Mac and taught myself how to use voice recognition and to type with one hand. I researched brands of gear I would need for the different climates I'd encounter. My current wardrobe was completely tailored to the perpetually summerlike months in Florida, but I'd be facing freezing temperatures in cities like Minneapolis and Chicago, so I needed to buy a warm jacket and gloves. And I wanted to fit everything into a single backpack, which would be tricky.

Everything about the planning was a challenge, but I was constantly buoyed by messages from friends and former students.

My student Nikki Martinez wrote, "I pray that I can influence the lives of my students the way you've influenced mine. Thank you for all you've taught me and continue to teach me. I promise every student who leaves my classroom will know your name and the impact you had on my education. Happy adventuring, my friend, and know that my prayers and the prayers of so many others follow you wherever you go."

In late September, I did a test run. I flew into New Jersey to visit a friend, and then rode the train to New York to spend time with Jacques. The trip was a disaster—including a fall in a subway station that resulted in a broken arm—and I documented it with a post for my followers:

I came back from my test run to New York and New Jersey with a lot of information regarding my equipment and myself. In regards to my equipment, I learned that a twenty-pound pack is quite a bit heavier and more unwieldy than I thought it would be. I also came to realize that my new disabilities are going to take a bit more practice, focus, and discipline if I am going to experience and enjoy this trip for all it's worth. For instance, I now know I shouldn't walk into objects or fall down as much, as apparently those behaviors will result in a broken right forearm. That's OK, I needed more practice with my left anyway.

Words of support flooded in:

"Those bumps and bruises are just character. Keep it going!"

"Chicks dig scars!"

"You can do it, Mr. Menasche!"

I tried to make light of what had happened, but the truth is I was shaken by the experience. If I couldn't get around on a short trip—where most of my travel had been on a plane—how in the world was I going to navigate what was turning out to look like thirty or more cities all around the country, traveling on trains and buses? I paced around the house, thinking about all the obstacles I'd face on the road, and wondering about leaving Paula and the house and the consequences of that. When I'd asked her to join me, she'd refused, saying, "I think we want different things out of life."

A few days later, another student posted a quote on my Facebook page from *To Kill a Mockingbird*. She had no way of knowing, but it was my favorite quote from the Harper Lee classic: "I wanted you to see what real courage is, instead of getting the idea that courage is a man with a gun in his hand. It's when you know you're licked before you begin, but you begin anyway and see it through no matter what."

Paula had been right. We did want different things. She needed to stay for the house and our pets and her job. I needed to take myself back and go.

My vision quest was one month away. If I didn't go now, when? I wasn't going to see any better tomorrow. My leg hurt, but at least I could still walk. Who knew for how long? It was time to stop listening to all the excuses in my head and see it through.

18

On Friday, November 2, right on schedule, I strapped on my backpack, grabbed my red-tipped cane, kissed Paula goodbye, and headed out. My plan had been to catch the no. 42 bus to the Metrorail and board a train for Tallahassee, where a group of my students were giving me a send-off party. But I was deeply grateful when my childhood friend Hilary Gerber, who was on her way to Tallahassee to visit friends, offered to drive me instead. Hilary had been my girlfriend in high school and we'd stayed in touch over the years. She is also a doctor, and as well as being my chauffeur for a day, she tended to my infected broken arm. Tossing my stuff into the back of Hilary's blue Mazda, I glanced one last time at the sign I'd painted and draped over the front porch railing. The words of Dylan Thomas: "Do not go gentle into that good night . . . Rage, rage against the dying of the light."

That was the plan. I knew the odds were that I'd die on the road from my illness. The doctors had told me that without treatment my chances of a tomorrow were slim at best, but I wasn't going to go gently.

"So how does it feel to be on the road?" Hilary asked once we were.

"Excited but anxious," I said. "There are still a lot of loose ends. But there's this feeling of 'Finally!' There was so much anticipation, so much planning and thought. Until this moment, I could only imagine how it would be. Now I can actually start putting things in my memory bank."

The drive from Miami to Tallahassee is around five hundred miles of mostly wide-open highway. As we headed north on the turnpike, I felt a kind of energy I hadn't felt in a very long time. Even if I didn't make it to my first stop, at least I had left. I hadn't given in to the cancer.

Hilary had to do all the driving, so at about the halfway point, near Orlando, we decided to stop for something to eat. On a whim, I posted on Facebook: "Hey everybody! I'm in Orlando at a place called Belle Isle Bayou. Meet me there!" We reserved a table for five, just in case. Within a couple of hours, our party had grown so large that we took up the entire restaurant. Looking around at the faces of former students now attending the nearby University of Central Florida, as well as friends from my youth who'd also shown up, I felt like a very lucky man, and I said as much in another post later that night: "So far the trip has been incredible!" To which one of my former students replied, "what is this trip about? r u trying to raise cancer awareness or sumthing? and how r u driving if ur blind and by urself?" I responded, "Nick, I'm worse at driving than you are at spelling. I'll be taking trains, buses, and catching rides." First lesson: I didn't need a classroom to continue being a teacher.

Next stop: Tallahassee. Dozens of students greeted me at a place called Club Episodes. The club is down the street from Florida State University, where a lot of Coral Reef graduates go. Walking in, I noticed that everyone was wearing the same T-shirt. The shirt had a picture of me wearing a surgical mask and giving the middle finger while receiving a round of chemotherapy with the words "David Menasche's Vision Quest" at the bottom and "Fuck Cancer" in an arc around the top. My sentiments exactly. It was surprisingly cold for Florida, forty degrees that night, but the love in that room warmed me.

"How are you feeling, Mr. Menasche?"

"I can't complain!"

"I miss you!"

"Miss you more."

"You were the best teacher I ever had."

"I loved all of you."

I was reminiscing with a group of my kids when I noticed a woman I knew but just couldn't place. After a few minutes, I walked over to her, a dozen or so former students trailing behind me. "I'm Jenny," she said. It took me a minute. "Oh my God! Jenny Armus!"

I first met Jenny when we were seven or eight. We attended Hebrew school together at Temple Israel in Miramar, Florida. Jenny moved away in the middle of seventh grade, but the next year she came back for Heather Brown's bat mitzvah and we'd kissed.

"I've never forgotten that night!" I cried, as my students formed a circle around Jenny and me.

"Me either," she said. "You were my first kiss!"

"Your first kiss! Are you serious?"

"Oh yes," she said. "I'm serious."

As I watched the reactions of my kids, I was reminded of the old Monty Python skit. *Nudge nudge. Wink wink.* They couldn't hear enough about their old teacher's young love life and hung on every word.

Jenny wasn't the only person there from my long-ago past. As she and I continued to share memories, Bleubird, my childhood next-door neighbor turned rapper, was now taking the stage. He instantly turned the night into a roast, telling lots of embarrassing stories I am happy that my students hadn't heard while still in my classroom: "He blew up my best friend's shoe with a firecracker. He gave me the courage to jump my launch ramp without kneepads. For some reason he had more patience with me than my brother and took it upon himself to toughen me up. He would don sparring pads and beat me up all over the front yard. Once he duct-taped pillows to me in an effort to teach me how to defend wooden ninja sword attacks! He was my teacher as well . . . I just got the young, uncensored version."

The night was magical. Coming into the club, I had worried about my students' reaction to me. Most had only ever known me as whole—a healthy-looking guy with a good head of hair and a stride in my step that exuded the confidence I'd once enjoyed. Now I was limping with a blind man's cane. The last thing I wanted was for my kids to think of me as pitiful. But if some were taken aback by my vulnerabilities, they pretended not to notice. I was smothered with gestures of appreciation and love.

It went by too fast. Before I knew it, it was time to leave.

As I was gathering up my things, a student ran up to me, her face red with worry. "Mr. Menasche!" she cried. "The police are here!"

"It's okay," I said. "No problem. I'll handle this."

I walked outside and introduced myself to the officers, who were just getting out of their squad car. "Is something wrong?" I asked. "No, sir," one of them said. "My name is Robert. You won't remember me, but ten years ago I was put into your honors English class by mistake. I was only in your class for a few days before they scheduled me into a regular class, but I never forgot you. When I heard you'd be here, I had to come by. May I take a picture with you?"

I didn't remember Robert, but I'll never forget his face again.

As the police car drove away, my students surrounded me in the parking lot. No one wanted the night to end, but I had to be up early to travel to my next stop, New Orleans.

"Hey!" I shouted. "Anyone got a couch for me tonight?" Everyone raised their hands.

I remember a regular lunchtime event was David chasing me around the lunch table. If memory serves me correctly, the goal was to make me "squeak" when he tickled me. Hence, my nickname became Squeaky. Over the years, each and every time I have been called Squeaky, I've thought of him and smiled.

I was glad I went. It gave me real insight into the man David had become. I was happy to see that he is well loved and well respected, someone who has grabbed life by the horns, not letting it pass him by, and teaching others to do the same.

As I said my good-bye, I was very heart-heavy. I felt we should have had more of a chance to talk to each other, but I was grateful for that small window of time we had been given after all those years. I kissed him on the cheek and hugged him good-bye.

—Jenny Armus,
Nova Middle School,
Davie, Florida

19

I had always been curious about New Orleans. How do you not wonder about a place that calls itself the City of Southern Decadence, a perpetual carnival with the best jazz musicians on the planet, nonstop gumbo and jambalaya, streetcars, the Mississippi River, and a collective earthiness that encourages grunge wear and a premier art event called Dirty Linen Night? It seemed to me that there was a lot to learn there. And a chance to be close to the place where Mark Twain wrote *The Adventures of Huckleberry Finn*, a book that had so inspired me as a young boy.

My former student Melissa Gomez, who had moved to New Orleans to study at Loyola University, offered me a couch in the house she shared with three roommates. I was hesitant to accept at first. I remembered Melissa as a hypersensitive and fragile kid, and I didn't want to burden her with the reality of my illness. Even though she had followed my plight on Facebook, I worried she wouldn't be able to handle seeing her teacher—someone she had frequently turned to for support for everything from boy problems to the SATs—as anything less than the rock I had been for her. But because my mission was to reclaim lost memories and find out whether I'd made a difference in my students' lives, I ended up accepting Melissa's offer.

I wasn't with her for half a day before I learned the valuable lesson that people do indeed change. Melissa had grown from an insecure high school student into someone with a clear vision of what she wanted from life.

She further blew me away by pinpointing her life change to an exact moment in class. "It started with you," Melissa said. She reminded me of the time, during her junior year, when she rushed into my classroom one morning before the bell rang, frantic because it was the last day to complete college applications and she hadn't even begun the process. I gave my other classes reading assignments while she and I sat together all day, filling out forms and discussing themes for her college essay.

"I was so nervous and anxious about not being adequate enough that I'd procrastinated about doing my college applications, but you made me feel like I was worth it," she said. "It may sound insignificant, but it got me where I am today."

I realized that Melissa had become a seeker. Having

risked leaving home at eighteen years old for a strange city where she didn't know anyone, she'd cultivated a life and many friendships in the time she'd been there. In her third year at Loyola, she planned to go on to Louisiana State University to pursue a graduate degree in social work. The little girl who was afraid of her own shadow was now a mature young woman with an altruistic spirit. "I want to spend my life helping people, the way you helped all of us," she said. "That's why I invited you to stay with me. You showed me the way in my path in life. I wanted to do something to help you on your journey."

For the next couple of days, Melissa played tour guide, showing me around her city, taking me on a streetcar tour of St. Charles Avenue and the French Quarter, and to the famous jazz clubs along historic Frenchmen Street. But what really touched me was that she welcomed me into her new life, introducing me to some of the colorful people she'd met since being there. The most interesting was a man named the Reverend Goat Carson.

I'd never heard of the Reverend Goat, but there's virtually no one in New Orleans who doesn't know the name. A local legend, he lives in a modest shotgun shack with peeling beige paint in a neighborhood where, seven years later, scraps of Hurricane Katrina continue to litter the landscape. Melissa reluctantly told me how she'd met him, which gave me pause. Strange things had been happening in her house, she said—things dropping off shelves and doors slamming in the middle of the night—and she and her roommates had gotten to the point where they were afraid to go to sleep. When they mentioned what was happening to a local, he suggested they go talk to Goat, a Cherokee Indian medicine man and shaman who knew ways to cleanse houses of bad spirits. The girls did, and Goat performed a ritual that apparently did the trick because the noises stopped. "I want you to meet him," Melissa said. "Um, okay," I replied. "I'm always up for a new experience."

Goat answered the door wearing red leather pants and a red cowboy hat bedazzled with shiny things. I later learned he was sixty-eight, but he looked older with his hair falling in a straggly ponytail to his backside. He looked like he'd lived a lot, but there was an unmistakable warmth about him and I was instantly happy I'd come.

You don't meet guys like Goat in Miami. His house told his story. Everything was a relic of his life, and most of the relics were tacked to the walls. A picture of him with the legendary musician Dr. John. Another one of Goat standing at a podium during his 1992 run for president of the United States. (His running mate was Eagles guitarist Joe Walsh; they got 100,000 votes.) A Native American Music Award (NAMA) for Best Spoken Word Recording. A citation for his songwriting contribution to Dr. John's Grammy Award–winning album *City That Care Forgot*. And what really got my—the English teacher's—attention, the cover of his published novel, *Shallow Graves*. ("I was trying to sleep it off when the smog crept through my window and started choking me. It was hot, much too hot to sleep. I tried to remember why I'd been drinking until 3 a.m. and whose funeral I had to attend today.")

I sat down on one of the animal pelts scattered around the living room, and Goat grabbed an instrument he called his harp—a buffalo's jawbone with strings that he'd made himself—and played us some of his music. At one point, he grimaced and said he'd been having some pain lately and wasn't sure what it was. I told him my story—about the cancer and the trip—and he shared with me that he was awaiting test results that could shed light on what was causing his pain.

Before I knew what was happening, Goaty, as his friends call him, had begun performing "a cleansing" on me. He draped my shoulders with a red shimmery jacket with big shoulder pads and placed eagle and turkey feathers all around me. Then he rolled a mixture of pot and sage into a leaf of paper, lit it, and waved it around the room. As he filled the space with smoke from the joint, the way a priest swings a censer of incense when he blesses an altar, he chanted in a Native American tongue. The jacket, Goaty explained, was the armor for my trip. The feathers were my talismans, to avert evil and bring good fortune. The smoke was used to clear any unwanted spirits from around me, and the chants were to cleanse me. Of what? I didn't ask, but I assumed it was the cancer. At least that's what I was hoping. Afterward, we shared the joint. I had been prescribed synthetic marijuana by doctors at Duke to control my daily nausea but, like others who use it for medicinal purposes, found that natural cannabis is much more effective. Goaty said it was all part of the ritual. I'm an open-minded guy. If this was a man who wanted to help, who was I to question his methods?

On my last day in New Orleans, Melissa took me to the bank of the Mississippi River, where we sat and talked for a long time. After a while, she opened up to me about a man she was involved with. She said she'd met him after he completed a stint in drug and alcohol rehab and that they'd enjoyed a good relationship until recently. Now she suspected he was using again. "What should I do?" she asked.

"If he's using again, you can either see this man as someone with a disease and try to get him to get help again, or you can believe that he is making a choice by using and seek something better for yourself," I replied.

Melissa smiled. "It really is black or white, isn't it?" she asked. "I've got to be in it or out of it."

I nodded. "I think so."

"If he's using, I'm going to break it off," she said.

"That's really smart," I said. "I'm proud of you."

"I'm proud of you, too," she said. "You've fought this disease for so long and you've been so brave."

"Thanks for that," I said. "But I'm afraid I'm well beyond my expiration date."

"Okay," she said, "but how many times did you already outlive what was supposed to be your date? I'm just sayin'."

I hated to see Melissa going through something so painful, but I was grateful to know that, even though we were no longer in the classroom, she still saw me as someone she could turn to for advice, someone she trusted. But even more rewarding was the realization that I trusted Melissa with being able to handle my illness. The girl I had once handled with kid gloves for fear she would shatter was now a woman who had the strength to encourage me.

As the sun fell, casting its orange shadow over the slow-moving water, the river seemed to have no end. For Huck Finn and his pal, Jim, the Mississippi was their lifeblood, carrying them toward freedom. That's how I felt at that moment—free, traveling toward my destiny, leaving my old life behind.

Alive.

I'm just sayin'.

20

I'd never felt as alone as I did hitchhiking in the rain somewhere in Nowhere, Alabama. I wasn't even supposed to be in Alabama. The day before, Melissa had very kindly offered to drive me the six-plus hours from New Orleans to my next stop, Atlanta. But somehow, and I'll never know how, we got headed north, and between the pouring rain and the pitch dark of the bayou, and with no GPS signal to help us get back on track, we ended up seven hours out of the way in, believe it or not, Tennessee.

With another seven-hour drive back to New Orleans ahead of her, and work the next day, Melissa took me as far as she could and reluctantly dropped me off at a cheap roadside motel with a red, flashing neon sign, somewhere in the boondocks north of Mobile. By then, it was late at night and I was just happy to have a pillow under my head.

It wasn't until I woke up the next morning that I noticed the rank smell in the room, along with the threadbare sheets, dirty carpet, and cigarette ashes in the sink. That wasn't the worst part.

When I went to the desk clerk to ask about a way out of there, she rubbed her eyes, smearing her blue eye shadow onto her cheeks, thought for a minute, and said there wasn't a train station or bus for miles and "Good luck, buster!" getting a taxi to come all the way out there. I wasn't too blind to see the handwriting on the wall, so I pulled on my backpack, grabbed my small rolling suitcase and my cane, and headed for the road.

Can I tell you how insulting it is to be limping with a cane, with your thumb out, and nobody stops? How threatening could I have looked? Frustrated, tired from walking, and feeling like a vagrant, I suddenly had an idea I thought might change my luck. I had taken to occasionally smoking medical marijuana to control my nausea and keep my appetite up, and someone in New Orleans had given me a joint to carry with me on my trip. I'd tucked it away in my backpack for safekeeping. As much as I hated to share it, I figured it might be a good bargaining tool on the road. If it got me a ride, I'd put up with the nausea it worked so well to suppress. As cars whizzed past, I pulled out the joint, lit it, and held it in my hitchhiking hand.

Not thirty seconds passed before I heard the loud

squealing of air brakes. A rumbling red eighteen-wheeler pulled to the side of the road in front of me. The passenger door flew open and I heard a voice shout, "You gonna share that?" When I was finally able to pull myself up into the truck, I was greeted by a spindly guy in his forties or fifties wearing a baseball cap pulled over his greasy blond hair. "Name's Teddy," he said, grinning and looking at the joint that was smoking in my hand. "DaVEED," I said, handing it over to him. "Nice to meet you, Teddy." He took a deep drag on the joint, then put the truck in gear, and we took off.

Teddy said he was headed to Pensacola and I decided to take the three-hour journey with him and then figure out how to get to Atlanta. He said he'd been driving for fifteen hours straight and by my best guess he was high as a kite. His knuckles were white from holding so tightly onto the steering wheel and he never stopped talking or gritting his teeth. This was certain to be the best roller-coaster ride I'd ever been on, I thought. Teddy was driving way over the speed limit to make his delivery on time and the rain had begun falling harder, making it difficult for him to see. Normally I would have been afraid, but the closer I got to dying, I found, the more adventuresome I became. Mark Twain said, "I do not fear death. I had been dead for billions and billions of years before I was born, and had not suffered the slightest inconvenience from it." I couldn't agree more.

Teddy asked me about the cane and I gave him a brief synopsis of my story. I asked him about the beer bottles rolling around by my feet. "Great story!" he said. The beer was called Mickey's Big Mouth, named for a former trucker, he said. Mickey created the wide-mouth screw-top bottle so truckers driving long hauls could drink the beer, pee in the bottles, and cap them without ever having to lose time for bathroom stops. "Clever," I said, taking a closer look at one of the bottles. It was only then I realized it wasn't beer in the bottles. The foul odor I smelled in the cab was bottled pee. Live and learn.

By the time we got to Pensacola (in record time, I think), I was worn out from the wild ride. I thanked Teddy for his hospitality and climbed down out of the cab. Teddy winked and nodded. "Hey, blind man!" he said. "You keep looking now, ya hear?"

I know you are alone, David. But I also know that my heart remains with you on your travels and my thoughts roam with you from state to state. I am proud to have known you as my best friend and will always hold dear our memories. Be strong and know you are never truly alone. Hundreds walk with you daily. I am but one. But my heart is heavy with your burdens. And my mind wanders with you as your feet wander the countryside. Keep us all posted. We need to know how you are and what you are doing. Write more. Express your experiences. Share with us. You are loved. Through and through.

—Denise Arnold,
English teacher,
Coral Reef Senior High School

21

I was about three weeks into my trip when Thanksgiving rolled around. It had been six years since my diagnosis, and in addition to being the anniversary of when my life changed, it was also the first time I'd ever missed spending the holiday with my family. The whole gang was gathered as they were every year, at my parents' house for my mother's traditional Thanksgiving meal, and I imagined everyone sitting around the long table, set with Mom's best china and crystal. Dad would be at the head of the table, with Mom seated next to him. My brothers and their families, as well as aunts, uncles, and cousins, would all be there as well. And Paula.

I'd been thinking a lot about Paula, wondering if she missed me as much as I missed her. But I didn't ask her about it when we spoke. And I didn't tell her that if she just said the word, I'd take the next train home to Miami. But she never said anything like that. She didn't say that the trip was too long or she wanted me home or she worried about me. Instead, she talked about her classes and her students and I told her stories from the road. At the end of every conversation I tried to convince myself that we were no different from every other married couple. And even if we were, then what? I didn't want to think about it.

I was on the Atlanta leg of my trip on the day of Thanksgiving, staying with my former student Karla Polo, her partner, Eric, and their two-year-old twin girls. We spent the bright, windy holiday afternoon at their neighborhood playground, and as I watched the twins play on the jungle gym from a nearby bench, I felt completely out of place. It was a beautiful family day filled with kites, balloons, and children's laughter, and I was the only one there without kids. I'd wanted to start a family ever since Paula and I had been married, but it was never the right time for her. Watching Karla feed her girls snacks and seeing how much they enjoyed one another's company, I felt saddened by the reality that I would never experience the bond between a parent and child. My chance for being a father was gone.

Eric must have noticed my sullen mood. He asked if I wanted to throw a football around and I happily accepted. But although I loved the idea of doing something to distract myself, I wasn't sure how well I'd play, considering my disabilities. It turned out that I could still throw pretty well with my right arm, but catching the ball was another story. Every time Eric tossed it my way, it bounced off my chest, and every attempt to run after it ended in an embarrassing tumble. It was beginning to feel like the entire day was meant to make me see firsthand what I was missing out on. But maybe that was the lesson—realizing what I was missing.

That evening, we all went to dinner at Karla's sister Claudia's beautiful home in a neighborhood of manicured lawns, where children played on the sidewalk and everyone parked in just the right spot. Their entire family was there and I listened silently as they chattered about neighbors and schools and in-laws and jobs—simple things that revealed how joined their lives were. After the meal, they put on a video of their recent family vacation to Disney World. I sat quietly, a dispassionate observer, feigning interest but secretly thinking about how good Mom's homemade stuffing with apples and cranberries would taste right then. And thinking that even though Karla's family was so kind and welcoming, I didn't even know all their names. *What am I doing here?* I asked myself, as the voices of Minnie and Mickey and gleeful children droned on and on. I felt fifteen million miles away from everything I knew and loved, and I might as well have been.

Looking at my watch, I realized that, at that moment, my family was probably sitting down to dinner, going around the table to each say what they were thankful for that year. I was thankful for a lot—for figuring out that I could still toss a ball, even if I couldn't catch it; for the thin line of vision that allowed me to see at least slivers of people and places; for all the love I was shown by so many old friends and the new friends I was making along the way. I wanted to take at least a moment to let my family know I was thinking about them, so I excused myself and called my parents' house in Florida. When Mom answered the phone, I could hear the joyful sounds of our family in the background. "It's not the same without you," she said. "How do you feel? When are you coming home?" The call lasted only a couple of minutes—I didn't want to keep her from her company—but it was long enough for me to miss my family in a way I never had before. *Note to self,* I thought. *Never leave home on Thanksgiving again!*

That night, back at Karla and Eric's, with the kids tucked into bed, we sat around the kitchen table, talking about the things that were happening in our lives. Eric began by telling me that he wanted to marry Karla, but she wasn't having it. Even though they were living together and had two children, Karla said she feared that marriage would rob her of her identity. I tried to consider both sides, although I couldn't help but wonder if either of them would think differently if they saw death on the horizon.

Watching Karla and Eric, I found myself envying their life together. There was something so intimate about the way they interacted. I'd never seen Paula look at me with the

intensity or passion I saw in Karla's eyes when she looked at
Eric. When was the last time I looked at Paula in the way
that Eric saw Karla? It struck me that my marriage to Paula
had for much longer than I had realized been more about
simple companionship than love. I was with Paula to avoid
being alone, because I feared not having someone to share
things with—the good and the bad. Yet there I was, experiencing people and places I could never have imagined before
I journeyed out of Florida, living on limited time, married
but alone. I'd always prided myself on my independence. I
didn't need anyone. Not me. Yet Karla and Eric clearly depended on each other and it felt natural and loving. I was
humbled to have to admit that being self-sufficient didn't
mean I didn't need love. I did, and I wanted to have it in my
life.

On my last morning there, when I was in the shower, a
jumbo-sized shampoo bottle slipped through my hand and
landed with a loud thud on the floor. Suddenly, Eric was
at the bathroom door. "David! David? Are you okay?" Talk
about feeling vulnerable. I'm in the shower naked and a vir-
tual stranger is standing in the doorway wanting to help me.
I assured Eric that everything was fine, but it took a couple
of hours before I could face him after that. Later, on the train
from Atlanta for Washington, DC, I began thinking about
how losing my sense of independence had made me feel like
less of a man. At the station in Atlanta, as Karla and I were

waiting for my train to arrive, a strong, cold wind had blown up, the kind that takes your breath away. I'd looked at Karla and caught the concern in her eyes. I knew what she was thinking. If it was that cold in Atlanta, what would it be like as I headed north? "Are you going to be okay?" she asked. I didn't have an answer. Until then, I had been with someone while traveling, never alone. Now I was on a fourteen-hour train ride, just me and my bedraggled body, nearly blind.

As I watched the Georgia countryside click by, it occurred to me that the people in Atlanta had accepted me disabilities and all, but did I? Why, when Eric rushed to my rescue in the shower, had I been embarrassed rather than grateful for his kindness and concern? The truth was, I was ashamed. I'd always trusted my own instincts above all else, and when I lost faith in my abilities and senses, I felt as though my body had betrayed me. Slowly, I began to miss the person I used to be and hate the person I had become. When my students suffered from low self-esteem because of something cosmetic, I would remind them that it was temporary. Their skin would clear up and their braces would come off, but I felt that I'd gotten to the point where life had stopped giving me things and had begun taking them away. My rational mind knew that having cancer is nothing to be ashamed of, but being sick made me feel weak, inconsequential, and impotent. This was why I wouldn't let Paula come with me to treatments—not because I didn't want to bother her, but because I didn't want her to see me as feeble and rotting.

I wanted to hang on to my sense of identity as a strong, resilient man. For my entire life, I had been so intent on never needing anyone that I'd never learned to trust people enough to allow myself to depend on *them*. Had I done that with Paula? Had I shut her out of my life by locking her out when I needed her most? By not trusting her enough to think she would want to stick by me? Had I run from her before she'd had the chance to run from me?

Fourteen hours alone on a train gives you a lot of time to think. As the Amtrak sped north, I realized that on my trip I *had* been allowing people to help me. I had been learning to trust. At every stop, I'd accepted support from my students and from complete strangers. It dawned on me that my world perspective was no longer appropriate for the man I now was. I wasn't a tough guy who needed to prove his manliness anymore. I didn't look the same. I couldn't do what I used to do. The David Menasche who once used the words of Jack Kerouac in *Lonesome Traveler* as his mantra—"No man should go through life without once experiencing healthy, even bored solitude in the wilderness, finding himself depending solely on himself and thereby learning his true and hidden strength"—was no longer with us. The new one was trying to find his way.

If I could accept the help of others, genuinely appreciative of the people who were offering it instead of being bitter, maybe that would mean I had accepted myself. I had come to terms a long time ago with the fact that I was going to die. My new lesson would be accepting that this was the way I was going to live.

22

I entrusted the conductor with helping me off the train at Union Station in Washington, DC. He seemed happy to give me a hand, and I was spared an embarrassing fall onto the platform. My former student Kim Kerrick had been one of the first people to respond to my Facebook post. She was driving four and a half hours from her home near Blacksburg, Virginia, to pick me up. That was a serious commitment on her part, which was one of the reasons I'd accepted her offer in the first place. Blacksburg wouldn't normally have been on my bucket list of places to see, but it was one of the visits I most looked forward to. Kim and I had been through a lot together.

It was rush hour in Washington when we left the station, and the city was tied in a tight knot of congestion. We sat in bumper-to-bumper traffic for an hour before we ever left the city limits for the long drive through the Blue Ridge Mountains back to Blacksburg, but the slow trip gave us a good chance to catch up.

When Kim had been in my class back in '06, she was a bitter young girl, cynical and defensive. Every comment someone made to her was taken as an insult, regardless of that person's actual intentions. She was constantly on the lookout for any perceived slight, and her own insecurities and shame were causing her to assume that others were against her when they really weren't.

I was therefore surprised when one day Kim volunteered to have her priority list read in front of the class, but I saw it as an opportunity to encourage her to become more open. When I read her list, I noted that "privacy" was listed next to "security," which combined with her depressed demeanor made me think that she might be hurting herself. In my experience, boys suffering from depression often turn that pain outward and tend to hurt others, but girls are more likely to turn it inward, as if to prove that the rest of the world can't hurt them as much as they can hurt themselves. It has, sadly, become an all-too-common way of dealing with teen depression and angst.

I sensed that Kim had fallen into this pattern. While I normally held conversations like this in the hall, in my urgency I crouched next to her desk and asked her in a private whisper, "Are you a cutter?" She said nothing in response, simply hanging her head in shame. At first, I thought this was because my words had rung true, but after thinking about it more, I remembered that Kim was a smoker. "No, you burn yourself, don't you?"

Once again, Kim said nothing, but the look of shock on her face told me that I had touched a nerve. After class that day, she lingered until all the other students had left. As it turned out, she was struggling with being gay and her mother's insistence that it was just a phase and she'd eventually "get better." "But I won't get better," Kim told me. "I know I'm gay. I've known for a very long time."

The following day, I asked Kim to stay after class, waiting for her to volunteer the truth. She said nothing and just stared at me. "You're hurting yourself, but how does that make the situation any better?" I asked, as she looked down into her lap. "You're only hurting yourself and your chances for inner peace and happiness." This seemed to get through a bit of her tough exterior, so I pushed a little harder. "You'll never be happy until you come to terms with yourself and proudly acknowledge who you really are."

The next time I saw Kim, she handed me a giant Ziploc bag filled with hundreds of matches and told me that she didn't need them anymore because she wasn't going to hurt herself again. Over the rest of the year, I watched her closely and saw her gain confidence as she came to terms with herself and her sexuality. She grew into a much warmer and more secure version of herself.

When he asked me if I was burning myself, I was blown away. How could he have known? But he did. Nobody had ever paid that much attention to me before. It was weird and kind of comforting that someone actually noticed. I started spending a lot of time hanging out in his classroom after that. He told me this story about a friend of his who went home for Thanksgiving and came out to his family. He was trying to let me know that it would work out. That I shouldn't be ashamed. This was something they needed to get used to, not me. He made me feel like it was okay to be who I was. It was encouraging because it gave me hope that my mom would listen some day.

He's still pretty much the same guy. His memory's a bit shoddy and he's a bit slower, but he's still got that same quick wit and badass attitude and that same extremely good heart. Can you believe his ringtone is "If I Only Had a Brain"? I only ever knew him as a teacher, but it was really great getting to know him as a friend.

—Kim Kerrick,
Coral Reef Senior High School,
Class of 2006

When Kim picked me up in Washington, it was the first time I'd seen her in over six years. She introduced me to her longtime partner, Mikilin. The three of us talked about jobs and daily life, but mostly, we talked about high school.

"When you were in my class, why did you volunteer to have your priority list read in front of the class when you had been hiding so many secrets?" I asked Kim.

"I guess I wanted someone to notice me," she said. "But I didn't expect you to keep noticing. That's why I gave you the matches."

"Because I noticed?"

"Yes," she said. "You were the one that cared enough to call me out on it in the first place. You were the one who encouraged me to try living, instead."

I asked her if she was still hurting herself.

"The day I gave you the matches was the last day I burned myself," she said.

Kim was no longer the brooding introvert I used to know. Over the course of the three days I spent with her and Mikilin, we had long and often personal discussions.

"You seem really happy," I said one morning, as we talked over steaming cups of coffee before she went to work at Starbucks, where she had recently been promoted to supervisor.

"I have a pretty great life today," she said. "I went to Miami-Dade and got my associate degree, then I transferred to UCF, but school was hard and I didn't finish. But it worked out. I wanted to get out of Florida. And I met Mikilin. Now we're talking about moving to California next year. We've been together for one year and nine months. Our friends say we're crazy for still celebrating the months, but we're just so happy."

Kim recounted her first date with Mikilin—at a Taco Bell—and we got a good laugh over that. "It was a horrible first meeting," she said. "Mikilin hardly spoke and I had to do all the talking!"

"Whose idea was Taco Bell?" I cried.

"Mine," she said.

"For a first date? Kim!"

"I know. I know. . . ."

I couldn't help but smile. The shy girl in my high school English class was now the person doing most of the talking. She had grown into her skin. And equally satisfying for me was hearing that Kim's family had accepted and embraced Mikilin as part of their daughter's life. They were all planning to spend the holidays together shortly after my visit.

Before leaving Blacksburg, the three of us visited Dixie Caverns in nearby Salem, Virginia. Traipsing together down 342 wet, dark stairs into the depths of a mountain was a dangerous but thrilling experience. Try that with a cane! Swarms of bats flew all around us, completely unafraid of humans. A bump from one nearly sent me tumbling down the stairs, but I caught myself, and once we made it to the bottom, we all relaxed a little. I was happy for the break. With every step I took, a hot needle of pain shot up the left side of my body from my foot to my ear, but I still smiled watching Kim and Mikilin enjoy themselves.

Excited to be doing something outside their routine, they sat huddled together, a picture of affection and love. Deep in the semidarkness of the cave, my eyes could barely make out Kim's smile, but I saw enough that I smiled, too.

Before heading back out onto the road, I asked Kim what would have been different for her if she had never dared to reveal her true self through her priority list. "There's a good chance I'd still be hurting myself," she said. "You definitely helped me open up." Kim's sexuality and even her self-mutilation did not end up shaming her once they were made public. Instead, confronting her shame and exposing her secret set her free.

The more distance I covered and the more people I saw, the more comfortable I got with who I now was. One night, on a train ride between cities, I remembered an essay by the inspirational writer Nancy Mairs that I used to assign to my class. The essay is called "On Being a Cripple." Of all the essays I had my AP students study, this was by far my favorite. I introduced the essay to my students by saying that I always hoped that if I ever had to face the hardships Ms. Mairs did, I would be able to deal with them with the same grace, humor, and stoicism. My own words haunted me as I took out my computer, looked up the essay, and began reading:

First, the matter of semantics. I am a cripple. I choose this word to name me. I choose from among several possibilities,

the most common of which are "handicapped" and "disabled."
I made the choice a number of years ago, without thinking,
unaware of my motives for doing so. Even now, I'm not sure
what those motives are, but I recognize that they are complex
and not entirely flattering. People—crippled or not—wince
at the word "cripple," as they do not at "handicapped" or "dis-
abled." Perhaps I want them to wince. I want them to see me
as a tough customer, one to whom the fates/gods/viruses have
not been kind, but who can face the brutal truth of her exis-
tence squarely. As a cripple, I swagger.

I wanted to swagger, too.

23

My parents owned a used bookstore, and while they gave me the gift of loving literature, the place wasn't exactly printing money. We always had what we needed, but not necessarily all that we wanted. At age twelve, I got my first job as a busboy, and from then on I worked many jobs in and out of the restaurant industry right up until my first day as a teacher. I worked hard to earn what I needed, but I never saw wealth as one of my main goals. In New York, I put myself through college as a bartender and made good money—more, in fact, than I ever made as a teacher—but there wasn't much that was satisfying about it. If I called in sick on any given night, another bartender would pour the drinks or another waiter would serve the food. Nobody cared or even noticed when I wasn't there.

Once I became a teacher, I found my fortune: one that

gave me fulfillment, pride, and a sense of purpose. In return I took every chance I got to instill in my students a desire to follow the path of their own dreams, even if it wasn't paved with gold. As their teacher, I wanted to see them happy in their endeavors, rather than just well paid. Since most people ultimately seek wealth in order to achieve happiness, money seemed like a middleman to me. Why hope that money would bring my kids happiness when it was feasible for their happiness to earn them money instead?

Sometimes when my kids were struggling to figure out what they wanted to do with their lives, I used a hypothetical exercise to illustrate that principle. I told them to imagine winning billions of dollars in the lottery. "I'm sure you'll want to go shopping first," I said, "and then travel around the world." I walked them through this scenario until we got to the point where they'd bought everything they'd ever wanted for themselves and everyone they loved and had seen all the beauty and wonders in the entire world. After all that, they still had an ungodly amount of money to spend, and I asked them what they would do to fill up their days. The responses varied widely. Some students struggled to come up with an answer, so I asked them leading questions such as, "You like taking pictures; how about that?" or "Is there something you'd like to accomplish in life or be known for?" Over the years, I heard everything from "I would want to teach kids to dance" to "I'd want to go to outer space," and all things in between. Finally, I asked them, "So if you would do that for free, wouldn't it be even better if someone paid you to do it?" I wanted my students to understand that, while money was important, it wasn't necessary to give up on their dreams to have it. I encouraged them to find a career that paid them while feeding their souls.

Of course, there were times when a student's more pragmatic family placed a high value on financial wealth and encouraged or commanded their kid to focus on a lucrative future. Anjalee Khemlanee was my student in 2001. She came from a strict Hindu background where financial success was seen as very important for men, but women were expected to marry for wealth. In high school, Anjalee begrudgingly accepted the fate dictated by her culture. She planned to become a housewife to a wealthy husband, but I could tell that deep inside the idea tore her apart. She had a great passion to see and experience more of the world, and I knew that a bright mind like hers also had a great deal to contribute.

During my exercise on wealth, I often introduced my students to a quote from Thoreau's *Walden*. "I would not have any one adopt *my* mode of living on any account; for, beside that before he has fairly learned it I may have found out another for myself, I desire that there may be as many different persons in the world as possible; but I would have each one be very careful to find out and pursue *his own* way, and not his father's or his mother's or his neighbor's instead. The youth may build or plant or sail, only let him not be hindered from doing that which he tells me he would like to do. It is by a mathematical point only that we are wise, as the sailor or the fugitive slave keeps the polestar in his eye; but that is sufficient guidance for all our life. We may not arrive at our port within a calculable period, but we would preserve the true course."

During our private talks, I pushed Anjalee to think beyond her family's expectations, saying, "You live in a free country and you should take advantage of that! What about pursuing your own way?" At first, I think Anjalee was slightly offended by my comments, taking them to mean that I didn't understand or respect her culture, but it was actually my deep respect for Anjalee that inspired me to encourage her.

I always wondered whether Anjalee would submit to a life of domesticity if she got a taste of what the rest of the world had to offer. I got my answer when I visited her in Atlantic City on the northeastern leg of my trip in early December, just a few weeks after superstorm Sandy hurled its wrath upon the New Jersey shoreline.

Anjalee was twenty-five by then and had grown into the type of refined Indian beauty one might find in a Ravi Varma portrait. She had recently moved from Florida to New Jersey to be a reporter for the *Press of Atlantic City*. I knew that journalists, at least the good ones, were driven more by passion and curiosity than by money, and I learned right away that Anjalee was one of the good ones. "I want to be in places where people can tell me something different," she told me over the noise of slot machines paying out gamblers one night at a glitzy boardwalk bar. "I want them to share their perspective on life. I seek out those stories, not the common community stories. I want to know the things that make people tick and make this world tick."

I've always admired the way good journalists are unwilling to have their news spun by others and instead become the lens through which the rest of us view the world. This is what Anjalee did every day, and her experiences as a reporter had afforded her a wealth of understanding and sophistication. After graduating from the University of Florida, she worked at a small weekly in Jacksonville Beach, Florida. "But I wasn't getting to do the stories that made a difference," she said. "So I applied to the *Press* and a month later I got the phone call."

We talked for so long that first night that the waitress kept interrupting us to ask if we were okay. "Couldn't be better!" I said. As I sipped a whiskey, my former student told me stories from her beat covering Pleasantville, a city within Atlantic City where one in five people live in poverty amid a blistering crime rate. "You wouldn't believe the crazy reasons people give for murder!" she said. Listening to her speak, I sat in awe. I'd longed to become a student myself on my trip, and I had found an inspiring friend and teacher in Anjalee.

We continued our conversation the following afternoon at her place. She lives in a sparse, unfurnished one-room studio apartment on the Atlantic City Boardwalk, with decadent hotels and casinos in one direction and the despair of the city's homeless in the other—a bird's-eye perspective on the greatest riches and deepest sorrows of life.

"You get sent out into the world!" I said. "It's a humbling thing to be a reporter, to gaze in on other people's lives, which you cannot fully know, and then relay what you find back to the rest of us where our only impression is . . ."

"I know," she said, "what I write."

"You are informing us. We are depending on you. That's a big responsibility."

"It's made me a bit cynical," she said. "I don't believe a lot of what *I* read anymore. So many journalists don't really do their jobs. They're more interested in their own opinions and ask only the questions that will get them to the answer they want."

"So, you have to sort out the people you trust," I said.

"Yes," she said. "And I need to make sure that what I write is honest and accurate so people can trust me. But enough about me," she said, turning on her journalist self, "tell me about your trip, Menasche. I have a ton of questions."

"Well, it has certainly thrown my life into this kind of

beautiful turmoil," I answered. "I live at everyone else's whim. The only thing I have control over is when I blow town, and I don't always have control over that. I missed my train coming here, had to get another one. It's a very different existence from when I was a teacher and I was in control. I decided what we would learn, and how to go about it, and how much time we would spend on it. I always knew what we were going to do in class the next day. Now I don't know my future past our talk right now. I have no idea what happens tomorrow."

"Is that scary?" she asked.

"Terrifying," I admitted. "That is the reason I don't want to go places where I only know one person, because if that person flakes on me . . . And people have flaked on me. In New Jersey, for example, three offered and you're the only one who responded when I got to town."

Anjalee's face hardened. "What?" she asked. "How does someone do that?"

"Because it was easy on Facebook two months ago to say, 'Yeah! Come on by!' But when all of a sudden a blind, crippled guy calls to say, 'Okay, what are you up to?' that's when it gets real. People say, 'Oh, gotta go out of town for work,' or 'The kid is sick.' The excuses start. Or they just don't respond at all. But it's all okay."

"No!" she cried. "No! It's not okay. Teaching is such a thankless job. It's such a shitty situation not to know whether you got through to a kid. Kids come and go and you have no idea who picked up on what. This trip was your way of—"

"—That's true," I said. "When I was teaching AP English, there was an exam at the end of the year. I would wait for those test scores and use them to judge not the students but me. If my kids did poorly, I'd failed."

"But that has nothing to do with you!" she protested.

"It has *everything* to do with me," I said. "Everything. If I can rejoice in your victories, I have to share in your defeats."

"But I was one of those kids who wasn't the best student, and—"

"That's where the teacher comes in," I said. "It's the teacher's job to make the kids care enough to want to do well. I never saw my kids as receptacles of my dogma, of my theories, of my views. I just put things out there and did my best to make it interesting enough that you wanted to learn more. A good teacher isn't about the content. It's far more important that you get the idea across—that you express it in such a way that it makes sense to your students. That was my gift, if I ever had one: I knew how to get it to make sense for you."

Anjalee smiled. "That leads me to my next question," she said. "Did you learn that or was that your personality?"

The young journalist was really good at her job. I thought for a moment before answering the question. "I never hit a point where I got tired of teaching," I said. "I was so tremendously honored to be there. For whatever small part I played,

I got to be there. And I appreciated that. I tried to please my students and I think they wanted to please me in return by doing the best that they could."

"Where did that idea come from?" Anjalee asked.

"I don't know," I said. "I really don't. But it's the only one I had."

When I left Atlantic City, I knew I would keep in touch with Anjalee. I had always believed that it isn't the person who has little that is poor, but the person who always desires more. Teaching by example, Anjalee completely disproved that for me. Here was a young woman who wanted more experiences in order to open up further opportunities for herself and to make a greater difference in the world.

———

I had a somewhat unique problem—one shared by those who come from very traditional ethnic backgrounds where women aren't supported in having careers. I knew I wanted to have a full-time job as an adult but was always faced with a time-line. In high school I thought I would work, earn big until I was twenty-five, and then "marry (a wealthy businessman selected by my parents) and settle down." I thought as long as I was able to earn and save some money, I could enjoy a bit of traveling before the chains of life tied me down.

I didn't think I could choose my own life, but many things—time and circumstance—helped me reach where I am today. I am a journalist because of Menasche, though. Rather than pursuing big money, I picked something I would be (and am) happy doing. I remember him being insistent that it was possible for me to have a career. He told me this at a time when I envisioned having my second child by the time I reached the age I am today. He used to say that I lived in a free country and I should take advantage of that. And I used to feel insulted that he didn't "get it." I remember defending tradition and respect for it—and my family. Now I've changed and balanced both. So thank you, Menasche, for insisting. For planting that seed in the back of my head. You were the first person to tell me something like that. Others came along after you, watering that seed. And here I am today.

—Anjalee Khemlanee,
Coral Reef Senior High School,
Class of 2005

24

I'd been on the road for more than forty days and visited students in more than fifteen cities, but I'd never felt as vulnerable as I did sitting in the Atlantic City bus terminal, waiting for my ride to New York. My cane rested on the seat next to me and my backpack was at my feet when I noticed the man sitting on my other side with three teardrop tattoos on his face. I knew that was a sign of having been in prison, so my antenna went up, especially when I saw him eyeing my bag.

The man leaned into me, a little too close for comfort. "What's with the stick?" he asked. "It's my cane," I replied. "I don't see very well." He hesitated for a moment, as if considering what I'd said. "Ain't you worried about it?" he asked. "Worried about what?" The guy was beginning to make me nervous. "Telling everybody that you're not gonna recognize them in a police lineup." *Okay*, I said to myself, *I think you're being threatened*. My right hand slowly inched its way toward the knife on my belt, which I carried with me on my trip to protect me from potential situations like this. My friend saw the knife and immediately jumped up. "Whoa, young blood, we don't need that," he yelled. "So we're cool?" I responded. "Yeah, we're cool," he said.

I was becoming a seasoned drifter. Nobody was going to take advantage of me if I could help it. But I still wasn't hardened enough to deal well with the Greyhound bus ride into Manhattan in bumper-to-bumper traffic. The jerky, stop-and-go two-hour ride was hell on my body. And the moldy, old-refrigerator smell of the bus didn't exactly help matters. I vowed to stick to trains after the experience.

I was feeling pretty fragile when I arrived at Manhattan's Port Authority on December 12 and set out to meet a group of former students at a bar called Kettle of Fish in Greenwich Village. At first I was doing fine navigating my way around, but then I got confused about the location of Christopher Street and couldn't see the street signs well enough to read them. I managed to spot a woman standing on the corner playing with her cell phone.

"Excuse me. Which way is Christopher?" I asked.

"That way," she said. She must have pointed, but I didn't see it.

"I'm sorry, which way?" I asked again.

I guess she saw my cane and realized I might need more help. "Do you want me to walk you?" she asked.

"No, just point me in the right direction," I said.

I felt her hands on my shoulders as she pivoted me in the direction of Christopher. "It's that way," she said.

I thanked her and took two steps into traffic when I heard her again. "Stop! Oh, just let me walk you!" she cried as she ran over and grabbed my left arm.

"Thank you. My name's David," I said.

"Hi," she said in a singsongy voice. "I'm Jessica."

We chatted amiably as she walked me across the street and then down the block to the bar. One of my former students, Sergio Noriega, was waiting for me out front.

"Sergio, Jessica," I said. "Jessica, Sergio." They shook hands and she gave me a peck on the cheek and then was off.

"Do you know her?" Sergio asked in disbelief.

"No. I just met her over there," I said, pointing.

"I recognize her from TV!" he gushed. "From that sex show!"

The woman who had come to my aid, I learned, was none other than Sarah Jessica Parker, the world-famous star of *Sex and the City*. And here I'd been worried that I'd end up getting taking advantage of (or worse) by a stranger. Instead I'd been helped by one of the city's most famous residents. Even better, I managed to avoid getting hit by a taxi.

I was happy to see that my former student Aaron

Rawcliffe was among the students who were waiting to greet me at the Greenwich Village bar. Aaron was the student who showed up drunk on my very first day of teaching back in 1997. He was in his thirties now and I didn't recognize him at first, but he turned out to be my saving grace that night. He offered me a couch in his Queens apartment.

In high school, Aaron had long, greasy hair and his wardrobe consisted of grungy jeans and Ozzy Osbourne concert T-shirts. Now he had an expensive haircut and wore shiny leather shoes and a business suit.

"Don't judge me!" he cried when he saw me. "I'm just coming from work."

"Look at you!" I said, embracing my old student. "You look like an executive."

Aaron *was* an executive, for a technology firm in the city. He filled me in on his path from Miami to New York. "My attitude has changed from back then," he said. "I used to rebel against the system. But I've come to embrace it and used it to my advantage."

Aaron said that after high school he went directly into the workforce, as a teller in a bank around the block from Coral Reef. "I fought with my bosses a lot," he said. "I showed up to work with blue hair! I was always trying to grab attention any way I could get it." That was the Aaron I knew. This young man looked the polar opposite. "One day," he said, "I looked in the mirror and I said, 'I'm never going anywhere in life if I stay on this path.' So I resigned from the bank, went back to school, and went into the tech industry."

"And now you're a businessman!" I said.

Aaron was full of surprises. I had expected he'd be living in a hostel. But his apartment was spacious and modern with plenty of glass and not a speck of dust. It was an adult home, not the crash pad I'd imagined.

When we sat at his kitchen table, Aaron pulled up his pant leg to show me that my old student hadn't completely abandoned his old ways. Under the tailored gray pants was a leg covered with tattoos of Ozzy Osbourne album covers. Osbourne had been his favorite musician when he was back at Coral Reef. "Still is!" he said brightly. He played his metal CDs and we spent hours talking about concerts he'd recently been to and comparing tattoos. I showed him the newest one I had on my chest: "I Decide."

Aaron has the memory of an elephant, and listening to him recount stories from the classroom during our visit gave me back memories I thought I'd lost forever. We talked about the journals I had my students keep: he still had his somewhere, he said. He remembered writing exercises I'd completely forgotten about and names of students that had gotten lost in my head.

I felt like I got to know Aaron all over again. He was as intellectually independent as he was in high school, but he'd earned the financial independence to go along with it.

He was a walking contradiction—yuppie by day, radical by night—but it worked for him.

I guess it shouldn't have surprised me that so many of my former students living in New York, one of the richest cities in the world, were doing well financially. After leaving Aaron, I went out to Brooklyn to visit Alfonso Duro, who was probably the wealthiest of them all. In high school, Alfonso was athletic and smart. I would describe him as "All-American," except for the fact that he came from Spain and was still a bit insecure about his thick accent. It was in my class that Alfonso read his first adult novel, *Huckleberry Finn*. He really responded to the deeper meanings of the book; I could see his mind kicking into a new gear. Alfonso became not only a voracious reader throughout the year but also a skilled writer. By the time he graduated, he'd decided that he wanted to be a sports journalist.

As an athlete, Alfonso already had his foot in the door, and after college he immediately found work as a sportswriter. I kept in touch with him over the years, and I remember him telling me by email that he was moving to New York City to take a job as a journalist for Microsoft. He had found a way to make money while living his dream, but his contract was only for one year. He knew he'd have to find a higher-paying job in order to be able to afford to stay in New York. Eventually, he landed a job in the advertising department at Microsoft and transferred to Google a few years later.

By the time we reunited on my trip, Alfonso was a high-level executive at Google. I'd be lying if I said that I wasn't impressed by the capital he had amassed, including two Brooklyn lofts with magnificent furnishings and a property in Florida. When we sat down to talk, though, I could tell that something was missing. Alfonso admitted that while he liked working at Google and was certainly enjoying the money he made, he found little gratification in his work, which mostly involved designing pop-up ads.

"I spend my days creating things that people hate, that bother them," he said, shaking his head. "I always think back to things that I learned in your class, lessons like not to settle, to do what you want to do."

Was Alfonso really settling? He and his wife were talking about buying the entire building in which they already owned the lofts. But Alfonso had even bigger plans, he said. Over the past year, he'd started to pick up freelance writing jobs again, and his new goal was to become a full-time freelance writer. "The overall future path that I see for myself is something that you really impressed on me," he said. "Doing what I do now, I can make a good living and be very successful. Being a freelancer, probably not, but at the end of the day, what's money?"

I thought a lot about money during my trip. The times in my life when I've felt wealthy never had anything to do with the state of my finances. Except for the gear for this trip, I couldn't even remember the last time I'd bought something new. Now I was content to know that I would trade all the money in the world for this opportunity to be able to contest my death sentence for a brief moment while being on the road.

Before leaving New York, I visited with Stephen Palahach. My enduring memories of Stephen from his time in my classroom are of his great discussions about the meaning of love during our reading of Shakespeare's *Romeo and Juliet*. I can't be the only teacher to have thought that a story about two kids who disobey their parents, have a torrid love affair, and end up dead is an odd choice for required freshman reading, but I went with it that year. To help the students get into the story, we'd read passages, then I'd ask them how they might react if they were facing similar circumstances. One day, we were dissecting the balcony scene ("O Romeo, Romeo, wherefore art thou Romeo? / Deny thy father and refuse thy name, / Or if thou wilt not, be but sworn my love, / And I'll no longer be a Capulet."), and that led to a discussion about love. Although love is something the kids were all clearly familiar with, they used the word so frequently and to describe so many feelings and situations that it somehow lost its meaning. Many of them struggled to find an all-encompassing definition for love, something safe and reductive. Some of the more empirical thinkers wondered, "What is love . . . to me?"

Stephen was one of those students. Artistic and introspective, he was mature well beyond his fourteen years. That year at Coral Reef he was smitten with a fellow student, the school's beautiful wild child, Francesca Contreras. In the midst of our conversation about love, he raised his hand and asked, "What if you're simply happy knowing that someone you care deeply about is happy, and you're content with that?"

I replied that, at least to me, real love wasn't a noun, it was a verb. "Love isn't a feeling that occupies you while you sit on the sidelines, watching and waiting," I said. "It's a feeling so strong that it thrusts you into action. However, what you're talking about is one of the most painful feelings there is. You're talking about *unrequited* love."

Not long after, Stephen sat in my classroom at lunchtime with a few other students and the subject of love came up again. I told them love was like a match. When you first light one, it burns beautiful and wild, full of crazy passion and spark. Then relationships, like a match, catch a stable groove. You can watch a match burn steadily for a while, but eventually it will flicker, and it's then that you must take action. You can put it out, stoke the flame, or light another match and start anew, but your love must compel you to do something. The students asked me about my relationship with Paula, whom I frequently spoke about with great affection and pride. I described to them the way I acted when we were together, always walking a little bit behind her with my hand protectively on her lower back. Stephen smiled like he was picturing himself walking alongside someone special in his head. "Yeah, that's love," he said. "That's love in action."

When I reunited with Stephen in New York City, I was able to see the way he'd come to define love since high school. He'd discovered a love of writing and honed his interest into a real craft, over the years developing the confidence to write extensively and launch a career as a fledgling screenwriter. Once having taken that plunge, he couldn't stop pushing to discover how far he could take his ideas. Waiting for his career to take off, Stephen took a night job as a barback at a posh cocktail bar. Rather than just stocking the bar and replenishing the glasses for the bartenders, he embraced what he called "the paradoxical silliness and beauty" of carefully re-creating drinks from over a hundred years ago and had become quite good at it. During my visit, he concocted one of these drinks for me—a Sazerac cocktail containing absinthe, bitters, and rye whiskey—as we talked about old times and his new interests.

Over the course of the evening we spent in Stephen's artfully decorated Williamsburg apartment, I looked over his eclectic film collection with his adorably witty girlfriend, Carolyn. As the three of us talked about our mutual love of gritty crime films, the depth of Stephen's passion and knowledge astonished me. I was even more impressed, though, with how in sync he and Carolyn seemed to be. Stephen held her hand while Carolyn looked into his eyes brightly and finished his sentences with hilariously snarky remarks. They were relaxed with each other, yet the energy between them was alive.

My conversation with Stephen was more heady than personal, but I deeply enjoyed learning new things from him. When I told him my story about the first time I saw *Reservoir Dogs*, in New York at the Angelica Theater in 1992 while hosting two very sheltered and squeamish Swedish au pairs (don't ask!), Stephen jumped in to add that Quentin Tarantino's production company is called A Band Apart, in honor of Jean-Luc Godard's classic New Wave film *Bande à part*.

"Have you ever seen it?" he asked. When I confessed that I had not, he streamed the movie on his computer and the three of us huddled together on his overstuffed couch, talking, drinking Sazeracs, and watching 1960s film noir.

It was a perfect evening until, toward the end, I started feeling sick. Before and during the trip I'd experience severe bouts of nausea at least twice a day. When it happens, I feel a chalky sensation in my mouth as it fills with a metallic flavor, and then chills overcome me despite the fact that I'm sweating. I know to find a place to lie down and close my eyes until it passes. When it happened at Stephen's, I lay on the couch and didn't wake up until morning.

By the time I got up, Stephen and his girlfriend had

already left and I found myself with a fluffy pillow behind my head and a warm flannel blanket covering me. When I looked down, I noticed that I was wearing cozy pajamas that didn't belong to me. I smiled to myself, thinking, *Now, that's love in action.*

Two years after [the class discussion about Romeo and Juliet*], Francesca and I fell madly for each other and for a brief six months we brought each other happiness. I still had lofty, sketchy notions on the subject of love at the time. If Menasche had again asked me that broad question—"What is love?" I think I would have still been at a loss, searching for deferred feelings to define something I had perhaps not felt for anyone outside of my own family.*

There was, however, a situation he described that reso-nated deeply with me. It wasn't part of a dramatic classroom discussion. I recall it must have been during a lunch break and a few of us were talking to him about what he was like with Paula. He described how he was essentially on alert at all times, walking behind her a little bit, making sure she was never in danger. I thought about how she must not even be aware of this, how it was an act of an unconditional kind of caring.

For most people, the more painful, scary aspects of life re-main in this sort of dark area of human existence. Menasche is not only looking into the darkness, but also deliberately walking through it, into the unknown. I perceive that as heroic and also another kind of act of love for life, for others.

—*Stephen Palahach,*
Coral Reef Senior High School,
Class of 2006

25

I think of my tattoos as a way of using my body to express myself. Almost like visual poetry. With my custom tattoos, nobody in this world has a body that looks like mine, and each one tells a story about my individual beliefs and experiences. Whether it's the simple, stark, black 45-rpm record adapter on my left forearm that commemorates my friendship with my boyhood buddies or the sugar skulls on my right forearm, my ink, like my scars, reveals a bit of what lies beneath my skin.

On my left leg is the first tattoo I ever got, and it is god-awful. When I was sixteen my friend Greg, who previously had tattooed only pigskin, tried out his art on me. He began with the outline of a tribal design I'd drawn, doing such a bad job that I insisted on taking over and shading it myself. But I didn't help much. It is uneven and kind of gray with spots missing here and there—a truly bad tattoo. In Miami, my students could get tattoos at the flea market where no one would ask for proof of age, but I'd tell them to at least think before they ink. "Don't get a tattoo that you'll regret later," I always told them. "Make sure there's a good story attached, because you're going to have to tell that story for the rest of your life."

In fact, despite the botched first attempt, there's only one tattoo that I truly regret. After my diagnosis, I was driving around with a friend, feeling antsy and bored. I'd been reading about the great philosopher Marcus Aurelius and the philosophy of the Stoics in hopes of learning how to bravely cope with my disease and overcome it, and when we came across a storefront called Hell City Tattoos, I impulsively decided to have the symbol of the Stoics, a burning flame, tattooed on the palm of my hand. You're not supposed to get the skin on your hands or feet tattooed, but I didn't know that at the time, and by that night it had already started to run and fade. I felt that I needed a redo of that tattoo's sentiment, so I had the words "Be Brave" tattooed on my right wrist, the spot on my body that's most often in my direct line of vision. Later, when it became obvious that the treatments hadn't worked, and the doctor was insisting that I go the experimental drug route, I added "I Decide" across my chest.

I think my favorite, though, is the tattoo I got on my back on the one-year anniversary of surviving cancer. It's the cover of the Modest Mouse album that came out at the time, a picture of a hot air balloon holding an anchor—an image of struggle and survival. As my trip was winding down, I felt as if I had really earned it.

After spending a quiet holiday with family and friends in New York, a kind of merging of Chanukah and Christmas, I was on the road again, this time to southern New England. Paula was at her mother's home in Vermont, where she'd spent Christmas, but when I asked if we could meet up, she said she didn't think it was a good idea. I've always been pretty intuitive, but apparently not about love. I was still hoping we could work things out—what better way than to ring in the New Year together? But Paula seemed to be drifting further and further away. So she returned home to Florida and I boarded a train for Providence, Rhode Island.

I arrived on Monday, December 31, on the heels of a blizzard that had blanketed the town in knee-deep snow. It was beautiful but frigid. My student Laura Dammann picked me up at the station. The snowbanks were so high that I felt like we were on a bobsled track driving back to her house.

Laura had been my student in 2006, the same year I was diagnosed, and toward the end of that school year her father was diagnosed with prostate cancer. When she introduced the two of us, I found I related to him on many levels. Paul had been ill for a while and had endured brain surgery about ten years prior to relieve symptoms of epilepsy. He was a burly bear of a man with a boisterous personality not too different from my own, and we exchanged jokes and stories without any self-pity from either of us. I had the sense that if anyone could beat cancer, it would be Paul.

I'd lost touch with Laura after she graduated, and I didn't know whether or not Paul was still alive. On our first day together, her mother and sister joined us at the house, and we all sat down to share some warm tea. Across the room, I saw a picture of Paul on the wall. "How is he?" I asked. They told me that he'd passed away about a year before. His health had deteriorated slowly and he'd lost his abilities one by one. Toward the end he was wearing diapers and waking up several times a night, calling out in pain. I felt awful that they had all gone through this and I felt guilty for standing in front of them alive and in relatively good health. More than anything, though, I felt like I was getting a glimpse at my own future.

The next day when Laura asked if I'd like to go sledding with her family at a nearby golf course, I jumped at the chance. Having lived in southern Florida for most of my life, I could count the times I'd ridden on a sled on one hand. And the only time I'd ever been on a golf course was when I was a teenager living in Florida and my friends and I hotwired a bunch of golf carts and drove them around one night.

The golf course in Providence had giant hills. We all took turns sledding on slick plastic disks that looked like garbage can covers and sent us spinning. I was only able to grasp it with my right hand, and during one of my turns I flipped over a bump and couldn't hold on. I flew up into the air and came down smack on the back of my head. As I made my way back to Laura, I could see the fear in her eyes. I probably had a mild concussion, judging from the throbbing sensation in my skull, but the best thing about knowing you're going to die is that you stop caring about minor things like that. Months before, I'd asked my doctor at the Duke University Hospital about smoking, and he said, "Even if you got lung cancer today, the brain cancer will probably kill you first. So smoke 'em if you got 'em."

That day, sledding was my nicotine, and I went down the hill again and again, eventually hitting my head one more time, but enjoying every moment with the same reckless abandon that had motivated me to take the trip in the first place. As the Mexican revolutionary Emiliano Zapata legendarily said, "Better to die on your feet than to live on your knees!"

With our hats encrusted in snow and our fingers and toes finally too frozen to move, we went back to the house. While Laura fetched us some tea, I noticed that she had a copy of *One Flew Over the Cuckoo's Nest* by Ken Kesey, one of my favorite books, on her bookshelf. My students always loved the novel, which was likely due partly to my own burning connection to it. I found countless lessons within the text, particularly related to the themes of my life: conformity, independence, and victory. Confined to a mental ward, the book's narrator, the Chief, fights against the evil Nurse Ratched to retain control of his mind. He does this by pretending to be deaf and unable to speak, a small victory but a victory nonetheless. When his friend McMurphy loses control of his own mind after undergoing a lobotomy, the Chief sets him free by smothering him to death and then frees himself by breaking through the window and escaping from the ward.

"I've had it since high school," Laura said, when I pointed out the book.

"Do you remember it much?" I asked.

"I still love the characters," she replied.

I told her a story I'd learned while researching the book before I taught it. The character of McMurphy has a tattoo of a two-pair poker hand consisting of black aces and eights, the same hand, the story goes, that Wild Bill Hickok was holding when he was shot dead on August 2—my birthday—in 1876. It's been called a dead man's hand in honor of Hickok ever since, and I'd had it had tattooed on my forearm before I left on my trip. I rolled up my sleeve to show her. "It represents my philosophy for living since my diagnosis," I told her. "You can't control the cards you're dealt, just how you play them."

I was a freshman in high school and I got pregnant. I called him and asked him what I should do. He told me I needed to sit down and tell my parents. I was terrified but it was good advice. I had a miscarriage after a month, but I continued to use his advice. I didn't lie to my parents after that. He was right. Giving them the chance to handle the truth made us even closer than we were.

—Laura Dammann,
Coral Reef Senior High School,
Class of 2008

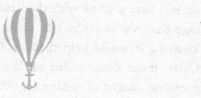

26

Before heading west toward California, I stopped in Boston to meet a few of my students there. It always amazed me that, wherever I went, kids made time for me in their busy lives on a moment's notice. I'd put out a call and someone always showed up. Boston was no different. I met up with Claire Contreras (who had been in my class), her sister, Francesca, and another former student, Martine Powers, at a bar near Copley Square. While they filled me in on their lives since high school, we noticed that the wooden table we were sitting at was all carved up with people's names, initials, and clever statements. I had the knife with me that I carried on my hip throughout my trip, so as we talked, I took it out and started carving into the table, etching the words, "I was here moments ago." The girls then each took a turn, with Francesca finishing up by carving, "Me too."

The first thing almost all my former students wanted to do was have a drink with their teacher. It was a rite of passage that was important to them and I always went along, knowing it would help them to feel comfortable with me. Often those times ended up lasting late into the night as everyone caught up with each other. It really was like having dozens of mini reunions and I loved every one of them. As we sipped our drinks, Claire began recalling her memory of me from fifteen years before. "You were very vibrant and lively and excited but also very dominant," she said. "I remember you pacing and speaking with a strong sense of urgency. You demanded we pay attention. Remember the Wite-Out thing? If someone fell asleep in the class, you'd go up and put Wite-Out on their nose." That was a memory better off forgotten, I said, and everyone laughed.

"You were the teacher everyone wanted," Francesca said. "Claire would always come home saying *Menasche this*, and *Menasche that*. 'Menasche introduced me to this guy Jack Kerouac,' and then she'd tell me about reading *On the Road*. She was really inspired and it occurred to me that I'd never been that impacted by a teacher and I was jealous."

I asked Martine what she remembered most from our class. "I was thinking about it on the way over here," she said. "Your English class was what made me think about writing. One of the first assignments you gave us was the pictorial biography and I loved doing it." I assigned the pictorial autobiography at the beginning of the year, asking students to include a picture and description of the ten most important moments in their lives. "When I did that, I started thinking everyone has narratives, even this thirteen-year-old girl. Each of those things on my list had a story. And I thought, If I have ten stories, other people have stories too."

Martine recalled how she'd once come to me and asked if she could write a story about a fellow student who was pregnant. She said she was surprised when I encouraged her to write the controversial piece, hoping it would help her classmates empathize with the pregnant girl's situation. As it turned out, the story was a hit with both the expectant mother and her classmates, opening Martine's eyes to her ability to touch others through writing. Ultimately she enrolled at Yale University knowing that she wanted to become a journalist.

Since graduating from college, she's been working at the *Boston Globe*, telling people's stories. "I love what I'm doing." Journalism, she explained, "is a really supportive community, a family of people who are really passionate about storytelling and the writing process. That's how you were. It was all about cadence and words that made the sentence pop."

I'll admit it. I loved hearing these stories. Even a dying guy needs his ego fed. And I was getting to hear things that are usually said only after someone is gone. As Shakespeare wrote in *Julius Caesar*, "The evil that men do lives after them; / The good is oft interred with their bones." I wanted to hear the good stuff before it was buried with me.

The next night, we all went out again, and my high school friend Ronnie, whom I'd kept in touch with but hadn't seen in years, joined us. Ronnie knew me as a person totally different from the teacher the girls still saw me as, but it was a great merging of worlds as we all bonded over drinks and laughs. Ronnie entertained my former students with embarrassing stories of me as a mischievous rebel with torn jeans and a skateboard, leading them to tell even more embarrassing stories of me in the classroom.

"I remember the time you broke the desk," Claire said. Trying to make a point to my class, I'd gotten so passionate about what I was saying that I slammed my fist on the desk and a leg fell off.

At the end of the evening, as we stood in the parking lot saying our good-byes, with everyone wishing me well on my long journey west, Paula called.

It had been two weeks since she'd spent Christmas with her family, and after an awkward moment of small talk, I could tell there was something she wanted to say but was having trouble starting. I tried to help her out.

"Do you miss me?" I asked.

She paused. "I miss telling you things," she said.

"Are you happier since I've left?"

"Well," she said, "there's a lot less stress. I'm getting a lot done."

"Do you want to make it permanent—without me there?"

"I don't know," she said.

"You don't *know*?"

There was a long silence. "I'll have to think about it," she said finally.

I waited a few days before calling Paula again. I was sick with anticipation over what she would decide. Being away from Paula, I had realized that I didn't want our marriage to end. For some reason, no matter how bleak the idea of reconciliation had seemed, it's what I'd been hoping for. We'd been together for twenty-three years and married for more than half of them, and we'd shared so much. I'd told myself that once I got back to Florida, we could work on what was wrong.

"I need to know, Paula," I said when she picked up the phone. "Do you want to make this permanent?"

"Yes. I think I do," she said, her voice quiet but strong.

I doubled over, like I'd been kicked in the gut. "This isn't what I want," I said. "Please . . . give me another chance."

She said, "I'm sorry. It's too late. You need more than I can give. When you come back from your trip, you'll need to find someplace else to live."

I felt as if I'd been left in the middle of a desert with no food or water. How does someone who is blind and crippled start over? I didn't want to know.

27

On the train ride to Chicago, I looked at my online "offer sheet" and didn't recognize the name of the student who had volunteered to take me in. I wracked my faulty brain for memories of the student, Danielle Lyew, but kept drawing a blank. I looked on Facebook in hopes of jogging my memory, but I still didn't remember her, so I proceeded to make plans without letting on, assuming the memories would come back once we were together. But when she picked me up from the Amtrak station, I saw only a stranger.

I was too embarrassed by what I took as my memory loss to ask her how she knew me, so I just got in her car and nodded along as she took me on a driving tour of Chicago. Over the next few hours, she showed me the Willis Tower, the Hancock Center, and Navy Pier on a crisp blue Lake Michigan before finally taking me back to her place. But even spending all that time with her hadn't stirred up any recollections. I felt terrible that Danielle had taken me in and shown me her city and I couldn't even remember who she was. After we had spent a day together, it was too late and I was too uncomfortable to admit the truth, but finally I hit upon a question that helped put the pieces together. "What do you remember reading when you were in my class?" I asked. "Oh, I went to Coral Reef, but I was never your student," Danielle answered calmly. "I heard about your trip from some friends and wanted to help."

The next day, Danielle told me that she'd always wanted to visit the Skydeck on top of the Willis Tower but hadn't felt she had the courage to until she heard my story. "You inspired me to take some chances and live life more fully," she said. Once she explained that it was a glass balcony jutting out from the tallest building in the Western Hemisphere, I was in. As my new friend and I rode the elevator to the 103rd story, our ears popped and our stomachs dropped. I was terrified as I gingerly stepped out onto the glass platform that loomed 1,350 feet above the minuscule cars that crept along Wacker Drive: I was literally and metaphorically on top of the world. In that exhilarating moment, I didn't have cancer; I had a friend, an adventure, and a tremendous feeling of self-determination and acceptance. I felt completely alive, healthy, and normal.

My stay in Chicago was brief. Before leaving, I also

met up with my former student Kaitlyn Flynn at a diner for grilled cheese sandwiches. Kaitlyn came from a devout Catholic family with strict morals, and so I was surprised in high school when on her priority list, she placed "privacy" next to "spirituality." She revealed to me in private that she had always felt ashamed of her Catholic upbringing because it was so far from the norm in Miami. That caused her to sit silently in class, perpetually afraid that her faith would be mocked by her classmates. She was deep but unwilling to share the true depth of her soul and spirituality with others.

I pushed my students to consider colleges far from home in order to find themselves away from the shadow of their high school selves, and I was always thrilled when one of them was brave enough to take that leap.

Kaitlyn was one of those students who took my advice and left Florida for college, traveling all the way to Saint Mary's College in Notre Dame, Indiana. Away from her family, in a smaller town, she felt free to reinvent herself and truly explore her religious beliefs on her own terms. She found herself going to confession several times a week. She began to find solace within the privacy of the confessional booth and was able to slowly begin to truly embrace her religion. After graduating from college, she had moved to Chicago and had made a good life for herself.

I was amazed by how much more confident and comfortable Kaitlyn was with herself than she'd been back in Miami.

She spoke at length about her faith, and I could sense that she had blossomed into a deeply spiritual young woman with an ironclad inner strength. On her own, she'd discovered that she was actually at her happiest when she was communing with God.

I was raised Jewish, but I've never been a religious person. My mother was born in a concentration camp during World War II, only months after her parents were taken from their home in Poland and separated. My grandfather quickly escaped and began working with the underground movement against the Nazis, while my pregnant grandmother was taken to a work camp in Russia. She was forced to make uniforms for the Nazi soldiers, and she and the other women had to meet quotas in order to get more than a few scraps of food. The other women secretly gave their food to my grandmother, often going hungry themselves, until the first day they met their quota, which was the day that my mother was born. Because the Yiddish word for "quota" is *norma*, Norma became my mother's first name.

While this story has a relatively happy ending—my mother and her parents all survived and were reunited shortly after the war—my mother's early childhood experience left her somewhat resentful of religion. She'd seen too much of what it could ultimately cost to ever view it as a wholly positive thing, and I think she passed that down to me.

What I do believe is that no God would be interested or

malicious enough to give me this disease. As Mairs wrote in her essay about being crippled, "I certainly don't like 'handicapped,' which implies that I have deliberately been put at a disadvantage, by whom I can't imagine (my God is not a Handicapper General)." To me, it's easier to believe that my tumor was the result of my own human doing somehow. I believe that God is in all of us. Divine intervention is within myself. I just needed to know how to tap into it. Who gave me the tools to understand how to do that? I don't know whether it was nature or my parents or society or God himself. Wherever it came from, it sustains me.

28

The temperature hovered in the single digits while I was in Chicago, and as I headed west it only got colder. With the train ride to Minneapolis scheduled to be a little over eight hours, I welcomed the opportunity to get off at the stops to stretch my legs. At one such stop, about halfway through the trip and in the middle of who knows where, I was standing a good distance from the train when the conductor called out, "All aboard!" By then, I knew the call usually meant "all aboard" within the next ten minutes, so I dawdled. I raised my cell phone to take a picture of the conductor as he stood in the doorway—it looked like a good shot—and just as I did, he started to shout at me: "What the hell are you doing out there? Get on the damn train!" Then, before I knew what was happening, the train started to pull away. I began hobbling as fast as I could, my cane swinging wildly back and forth—I'd left all my things on board—as the conductor threw me an icy look. Closing the distance to within a foot, I realized it was now or never, grabbed on to a metal handrail with my right arm, and with every last ounce of my strength swung myself onto the moving train.

Oh, but that wasn't the best part of the ride.

As the train continued on its path, with Minneapolis four hours away, I headed to the café car for some dinner. It was communal dining, and I plopped down next to a brawny guy who, it turned out, was headed to the Twin Cities for a weeklong ice-fishing expedition on Lake Calhoun. He reminded me of many people I met in the Midwest: cordial but not overly talkative. That was okay with me. Then my food came out—rubberized chicken—and, not being able to hold a fork and knife at the same time, I was having a hell of a time cutting it. With my one good hand, I rocked the knife back and forth on the meat in a pivoting action, trying to separate a bite-size portion, but I hardly made a dent. I was just about to give up when my ice fisherman friend suddenly spoke up. "Here," he said, pulling a gleaming silver hatchet from his pack, "let me help you." He raised the hatchet to shoulder level and then brought it down in one swift motion—*thwack!*—splitting my chicken breast perfectly in half. "Hm," I said, trying to act nonchalant. "Is that how you cut all your food?"

When I finally got off the train in Minneapolis, I took

a picture of the temperature: eighteen below. My old friend Jeffrey—I worked with him way back when both of us were waiters in New York—kindly offered to put me up. The next day, we drove out to Lake Calhoun to see if we could find my friend from the train, but the lake was vast and there were too many ice fishermen. Standing on the frozen lake in the frigid Minnesota outdoors, I looked around and wondered what kind of person enjoys hacking a hole in the ice and sitting there in subzero weather to catch a couple of fish? But I guess I had already met the answer.

Although I stayed with Jeffrey, I spent most of my short visit with a former student named Emelie. One of my students in my first year as a teacher, Emelie had confided in me then that she often felt lonely. Being so young at the time, and only a few years older than her, I felt out of my depth, too. So I told Emelie about a ritual I had of going outside shortly before midnight and looking at the moon. It always comforted me to know that no matter where I was or what I was going through, millions of other people were looking at the same moon at that very same moment. I told Emelie that if she did that, she would never be alone.

And that's what we did in Minneapolis.

After dinner and drinks at a local restaurant, we stood outside in the parking lot, talking about the places I'd been and the places she still wanted to go. Emelie admitted that there were times she still felt alone. I understood that feeling better now. Remembering my ritual, we both looked up at the sky—a teacher and his former student, each finding solace in the fact that, no matter where life took us, we could always look at the moon and find each other.

When I graduated high school you told me if I ever needed you, I could find you in the moon at night. Every day between ten and eleven p.m. you look out at the moon and I could find you there. There have been many times in the last eleven years that I have looked for you in the moon and found myself comforted.

Thank you for who you were to me back then and who you've been every day since. Your gentle and giving heart has touched the hearts of hundreds of others. I don't know how you do it. I always thought I was special. That you and I just had a special connection. But I realized you were the same Menasche to all of the other students who saw you the same way. With me will always be the words you wrote in my yearbook. I remember you told me you didn't know what you wanted to write. You wanted to just look at me and let the words come to you. You stared at me, didn't even look down at the paper, and started writing: "Here is a note to attempt to say all of the unsaid. An unspoken note of affection, bonding, and now longing. Perhaps the reason this is so hard to write is because I really don't want this to be good-bye. But as you know, all things must pass. Do your best to stay in touch. But

*I know I will miss you, Miss Lalama, I always will. Love, D.
Menasche."*

—Emelie Lalama,
Coral Reef Senior High School,
Class of 2000

29

On January 26, 2013, after a fifty-two-hour train ride that started in Minnesota and took me though the spectacular far north—North Dakota, Wyoming, and Washington—before turning south through Oregon, I arrived at my last state: California. It was an interminable ride, and the train was running late. I felt disoriented and stale as I disembarked, but then I heard "Menasche!" in a familiar melodic voice that put me right back into the classroom. When I turned, I saw my student Mona Tajali racing toward me. "Menasche!" she cried again, embracing me in a loving bear hug.

In the days when Mona was my student, she had just recently arrived in the United States with her mother, an Iranian political refugee, following the death of her brother at the hands of the regime. She had experienced the challenges women face in patriarchal societies firsthand, and although she had a strong female figure in her own household, she knew how women were expected to behave in her culture. As a young girl, Mona was rather submissive, remaining in the private sphere of the home. When she arrived in my class in 1997, she was very shy and struggling to reconcile her native culture with the expectations of a new country.

I understood why Mona connected to a short story we read called "The Yellow Wallpaper" by Charlotte Perkins Gilman. "The Yellow Wallpaper" is about a nineteenth-century woman who's confined for treatment of "hysteria," the term at the time for any type of female mental illness. As we discussed the piece, Mona saw, for perhaps the first time, a parallel experience to her own from the perspective of a Western woman also subjected to male dominance and patriarchy. The payoff of the book was that, in the end, this seemingly powerless woman triumphed over submission through her writing and her creative mind—her own intellectual independence that ultimately set her "free."

Today, Mona is happily married with an eight-month-old son, Benny, but she is also a PhD candidate, studying anthropology with a focus on women in Middle Eastern cultures. She works with an organization that writes and holds workshops about resistance against misogyny, raising awareness among women who want to improve their own status. She even coauthored a book on parliamentary gender quotas, which is currently being translated into five languages.

Mona drove me from the train station straight to Golden Gate Park. When I'd started out, three months earlier, my goal was to make it all the way across the country. If I could see the Pacific with the bit of vision I had left, I'd know I had succeeded. As I sat looking out at the majestic Golden Gate Bridge and the indigo-blue waters of the Pacific, as I had so many times in my dreams, I felt giddy, almost drunk with the purest sense of victory I'd ever felt. "I made it," I said. "I made it." And I had made it. I had succeeded in my goal to get my confidence back after cancer had stolen it from me.

The icing on the cake was having Mona standing next to me in that moment, the living embodiment of my greatest hopes and dreams for all my students.

———————

So thank you for all that you did. Thank you for welcoming me to this new environment and easing my transition to my teenage age and later adulthood, as I was struggling to find my own identity and figure out who I want to be. Thank you for your kindness and your care in our long chats about boys, friendships, parents, and college. Thank you for your encouragement for me to follow my dreams, no matter how many challenges lay ahead. Lastly, thank you for being a teacher in every sense of the word. I am so lucky to have had you as my teacher. You continue to teach, inspire, and encourage me. I am honored to have known you and thank you for coming and visiting me. Thank you, Menasche, I owe a lot to you!

—*Mona Tajali,*
Coral Reef Senior High School,
Class of 2001

―――――――

Before I left California, I had the opportunity to visit one last student—a girl so full of promise that I'd delayed my trip home to be able to connect with her. Aly Ocampo had been one of those kids who masked their potential with their insecurities and shyness. In class, she was often so overwhelmed by her own thoughts that she'd trip over her words, which led to her turning more and more inward. One day, we were in the middle of a mock debate and, in her haste to say something, Aly began stuttering and garbling her words. Some of the other students began snickering, and I shouted, "Pause the debate!" I ran outside to my car in the pouring rain and came back to the classroom a few minutes later, soaking wet and holding a red foam stress ball I'd gotten from the hospital during one of my chemo treatments. I handed the ball to Aly, who looked at me like I'd lost my marbles. "Squeeze the hell out of it," I said, "and then say what you want to say." What do you know? It worked like a charm.

For the rest of the year I kept the ball in my top desk drawer and handed it to Aly at the start of every class. She'd squeeze and squeeze until she was focused enough to speak. By the end of the school year, she was one of the most articulate students in honors English. Not long afterward, she was on her way to the prestigious Berklee College of Music in Boston. At graduation, I gave her the red stress ball as a token of my pride in her. "You may want this when you're writing your music," I said.

When Aly called and asked to see me while I was on the West Coast, I couldn't refuse. I delayed my trip home to meet her at her beautiful home in the Hollywood Hills. It turns out that Aly is earning an impressive living as the lead singer of a popular country band. She and her musician boyfriend, a guitar virtuoso named Josh, spend their time touring with their bands, recording music into the wee hours of the night, and hanging out with a fascinating group of artists and rock stars.

After our visit, Aly drove me to the airport. I was sad to see the trip come to an end and to part ways with another one of my students. To keep us both from feeling too down, I sang the theme from *Rawhide*—"Head 'em up, move 'em out, Rawhide!"—and held out my cane like a jousting lance as she pushed me in a wheelchair through the terminal. "You're gonna get us arrested!" she cried, and both of us burst out laughing.

The security people allowed Aly to push me right to my gate. Before parting ways, she reached into her handbag and pulled out the red stress ball. "I think I've moved five times since you gave me this and I still have it," she said. "Every now and then when I get really stressed or anxious, I still use it."

"Well, what do you know," I said. "What do you know."

My students had gone far in life, becoming husbands, wives, parents, Wall Street bankers, PhD candidates, government agents, immigration officials, writers, teachers, and lawyers. I couldn't help but think that I had been given the Golden Teacher Ticket. As a rookie just starting out, I had walked into one of the country's best high schools and, for fifteen years, had worked with students who were hungry to learn. On my trip, I had been able to stop being the teacher and become the student, and through my kids I learned about brand-new worlds and experiences. And most importantly to me, I got the opportunity to see in person the glimmers and traces that remain in each one of them from the time they spent in my classroom.

My students saw me now exactly as I am, painfully limping with a blind man's cane, accidentally stepping on their pets, bumping into their children, and knocking over their valuables. Despite this, they took me in, accepting me regardless of my condition and disabilities. With them, I was still their teacher, the guy they looked up to and thought of so fondly, and it was nice to be him again, if only for a short time.

When I returned to Florida briefly after my trip, I stopped in at the clinic to have the chemotherapy port in my chest flushed out, since it hadn't been used in months. This simple procedure would prevent me from getting an infection in the unnatural appliance that had been placed under my skin for injections back when I was getting treatments. My friend and former student Jennifer drove me to the all-too-familiar clinic, where I'd received chemotherapy sixteen times, for my appointment. Before going in, I warned her that not everybody in the chemotherapy suite had been a fan of my decision to quit treatments and hit the road. I wasn't sure what I would face in there, but as soon as we walked in, we heard the strangest sound coming from down the hall—applause.

"What's going on?" I asked, and Jen shrugged her shoulders as we walked down the hall toward the treatment room to investigate. As we entered, all the patients, nurses, and doctors in the room suddenly stood up as they continued applauding, and it took me a full minute to realize that they were applauding for me. Even the patients who could barely stand raised themselves up as far as they could, many of them throwing their arms around me or giving me high fives as I passed them. Finally, my favorite nurse, Sonya, presented me with a "Purple Heart Certificate" in recognition of my completing my trip.

When I had first decided to quit treatment and

leave—my equivalent of the Chief in *One Flew Over the Cuckoo's Nest* breaking through the window of the asylum and setting himself free—many people questioned my sanity. Now here they were applauding me for it. It's a moment I'll never forget.

Altogether I spent 101 days on the road, visited thirty-one cities, took 1,840 pictures, recorded sixty-two hours of audio, and met with seventy-five former students. Like Huckleberry Finn, I felt my worldview expand quite a bit during my travels. And like Huck, too, I found there "warn't no home like a raft."

30

From the porch of the house I currently call home I can see the moss-shaded road and the gothic houses behind it fading in the twilight. The sun is just setting on Prytania Street and on New Orleans—after a stretch of summer so hot and sticky that even my pink magnolias are wilting—and no one seems to be around. No traffic either. Instead a strange sort of silence envelops the neighborhood. It's a moment custom-made for reflection.

Only not for me. Leaning back in my lounge chair made out of skateboards, I can still feel the rush of movement of the train, the pull and push of the Greyhound bus, and the rough fabric of the dozens of couches I slept on. Being stationary, coming to a stop, taking stock, assessing lessons—all that hasn't hit me yet. People ask me all the time now, "How was your trip?" and each time they do, all I can think is *I'm still on it*.

Maybe that is a lesson in itself. Something about life being a journey whether you're aware you are moving or not. You are. I am. Everyone.

I firmly believed before I set out that I would die on the road. But I didn't. I *lived* on the road. It didn't kill me; it saved me. It brought me from the lowest point of my life to some of the highest. And what I found is that they are connected, the low and the high, that, as Bono sings, "If you want to kiss the sky, better learn how to kneel." Well, I kneeled. Time and time again, stumbling after a train or banging into someone on the platform, I was deeply and profoundly humbled—and frequently humiliated, too. But maybe I needed it. All along my motto had been "I've got this." A trip around the country, alone, crippled, and entirely dependent on the generosity of others, showed me I didn't.

At least not alone. And that's where my kids came in. They rescued me. From my early life as a skateboard punk with a bad attitude—and a worse haircut—they rescued me. And from my postteaching and newly disabled reality, with no job and no wife, they rescued me again. Literally thousands of them, sending me love and prayers and support, and hundreds spread out around the nation, dropping everything at a moment's notice to take me in. I literally don't know where I would have been without them.

Almost all the students I visited had memories of the priority list. Some still had their lists, five and ten years later, yellowed and crumpled and tucked into a high school year-book or an old journal, along with other precious vestiges of their pasts—a pressed rose, a graduation tassel, an old movie or concert ticket. Some of my students still return to the exercise every once in a while as a way of gauging who they are and what is important to them, at that moment in their lives. I told them what I said back when we were in the classroom. As life changes, so do our priorities.

After seeing so many places and meeting so many people, maybe it's time for me to reevaluate my own priorities.

I think my list now would begin with a word that isn't even on the original priority list. *Strength.* I used to confuse power (which is on the list) with strength, but I've learned there is a distinct difference between the two. Power is the ability to effect change. I wanted that in my youth, to have an effect, to make a difference, and I'm satisfied now that I used whatever power I did have well. But strength is endurance, so that would have to be near the top of my new priority list. Because all I ask for my remaining days is the strength to endure them.

What has not changed, what has stayed constant, before cancer and since, is my commitment to my students. They are my number one priority. But since my trip I have come to realize that I am their priority, too. I had hoped that as a teacher I would have instilled in my students a love of books and literature, and a deep curiosity about the world. What I got was something even more gratifying: I got students who grew up to be kind and loving people of the world. People who gave me shelter from the storm of cancer and of despair and didn't even need or expect to receive any thanks for it. If that isn't enough to renew your faith in people, I don't know what is.

The sun has almost disappeared now and the neighborhood has grown dark. But from behind me, from inside the house, there are lights. I can hear my roommates Jen and Melissa chatting and having a laugh in the living room before dinner. In a few minutes, when we sit down to eat, they'll help me twist the top off the hot sauce and maybe even cut my food. Once upon a time that would have seemed deeply sad to me. Now? Well, I feel blessed to have them around. And the fact that both of them are former students of mine—classes of 2009 and 2010—just makes it all that much more poignant, like a wheel coming full circle.

What I want to say is I owe all the happiness of my life to you. You have been entirely patient with me and incredibly good. I want to say that—everybody knows it. If anybody could have saved me it would have been you. Everything has gone from me but the certainty of your goodness.

—Virginia Woolf,
March 1941

CODA

> The greatest use of life is to spend it on something that
> outlasts it.
>
> —William James, philosopher

I saved a life today. Without doing anything extraordinary or
out of character, I saved the life of a student who had plans
to take her own life. By being her only voice of reason, offering grounded perspective, assuring unconditional acceptance,
and by providing her the safety of my cozy office, I saved her
life.

I am Kara Trucchio, a high school guidance counselor
and one of David Menasche's former students. I like to believe that it was my experience as his student that inspired
me to pursue my career in education. I was, and still am,
intrigued by Menasche's love for what he did. Teaching
was not his "job," it was his passion. Now that I have found

my own passion, I don't wake up every morning solely for myself; I have an entire student body dependent on my presence. Menasche, I sincerely hope you recognize your worth. I would be so lucky to even compare to your successes in inspiring students. You gave us the tools we needed as young adults to find our own passions. I feel we all have potential; sometimes it's just a matter of having the proper help finding it. You believed in every single one of us as unique individuals and instilled in us the desire to unlock the possibilities.

Menasche had a daily classroom activity that I never understood. Every class period, he asked us to keep a running list of random things that were said or done during class. For example: people who left the room, words that were said, questions that were asked, noises that were made. At the end of the class, we would compare lists. Only now, thirteen years later, do I understand. This seemingly insignificant activity taught me that there are things constantly happening around us that go unnoticed. It taught me to open my eyes to the little things. Life continues, the world turns, regardless of our individual differences and circumstances. I cannot help but relate this to Menasche's current situation. He has come face-to-face with his prognosis but has not let that stop him from living his life. Not everyone would be able to accept such a harsh reality.

Even though you stopped teaching, I continue to teach your lessons. I taught a few semesters of undergraduate psychology at a local college. I quickly learned that the textbooks and standard curriculum could not answer all my students' questions. Eventually, I found myself having to define the different types of love in my own words. Since this is close to impossible, I shared "Menasche's Eskimo analogy" with my class. Apparently Eskimos have hundreds of different words for snow because they have so many different uses for it. Why don't we have that many different words for love? I love my mom differently than I love ice cream. Love is a complex emotion, felt by everyone in some capacity. We are all capable of loving.

Loving, teaching, inspiring. Menasche, if you're seeking confirmation that you've touched lives, I assure you that you have. Your lessons and passion live in the hearts of your former students and forever friends. I promise to live a life of purpose and continue to pass on such inspiration to those who need it most. You most definitely have spent your life on something that outlasts it.

Acknowledgments

Thank you to my entire family for all your love, education, and support through the years. I hope I've somewhat redeemed myself for the trauma I put you through during my teenage years.

A huge thanks to my friends Heidi Goldstein, Toby Srebnik, and Hilary Gerber for making this trip—and by extension this book—a possibility. You've each played an instrumental role in my life and I'm grateful.

Thanks to every one of my students who either donated to my trip, offered me your home, or even just met me for a drink along the way. The time we spent together meant more to me than you can imagine. My time in the classroom with you was the most meaningful and fulfilling of my life up until the day I left for my trip. While I was on the road, you all showed me that my life was not over and that it could be even better. I will be eternally thankful to you for that.

I am so grateful to the team that helped put this book together. To my agent, Brandi Bowles, thank you for believing this could be a book and for all your support along the way. I couldn't ask for a smarter or more passionate and caring agent. Matthew Benjamin, thank you for your belief in me and for your insights about how to turn this trip into an actual book! Thank you to David Falk, Stacy Creamer, and the entire team at Touchstone and Simon & Schuster for all your help and support. Jodi Lipper, thank you for the hours of conversation that helped me to turn my personal thoughts into public prose. Robin Gaby Fisher, thank you for being not only a truly gifted writer and wonderful collaborator, but also caring, warm, and incredibly patient. I never could have done this without you, and the best part of this entire process has been getting to know you and being able to now call you a friend.

Thank you to every student who sat in my classroom over the years. I hope I was able to teach you even a fraction of what you taught me.

The Priority List

Acceptance

Adventure

Artistic Expression

Career

Education

Family

Friendship

Fun

Health

Honor

Independence

Love

Marriage

Possessions

Power

Privacy

Respect

Security

Sex

Shelter

Spirituality

Style

Technology

Travel

Victory

Wealth

About the Author

David Menasche grew up a punk skater kid with a love for literature and a lack of direction. He's careful never to say that he fell into teaching but that he "rose up to it." He taught English at Miami's magnet school, Coral Reef Senior High School, for fifteen yeras. In 2012, he was awarded Teacher of the Year by his region. He lives in New Orleans.